D0359686

The Art of Giving

Where *the* Soul Meets *a* Business Plan

Charles Bronfman
Jeffrey Solomon

Foreword by James Wolfensohn

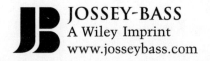

JOSSEY-BASS
A Wiley Imprint
www.josseybass.com

Published by Jossey-Bass
A Wiley Imprint
989 Market Street, San Francisco, CA 94103-1741—www.josseybass.com.

Readers should be aware that Internet Web sites offered as citations and/or sources for further information may have changed or disappeared between the time this was written and when it is read.

Limit of Liability/Disclaimer of Warranty: While the publisher and author have used their best efforts in preparing this book, they make no representations or warranties with respect to the accuracy or completeness of the contents of this book and specifically disclaim any implied warranties of merchantability or fitness for a particular purpose. No warranty may be created or extended by sales representatives or written sales materials. The advice and strategies contained herein may not be suitable for your situation. You should consult with a professional where appropriate. Neither the publisher nor author shall be liable for any loss of profit or any other commercial damages, including but not limited to special, incidental, consequential, or other damages.

Jossey-Bass books and products are available through most bookstores. To contact Jossey-Bass directly call our Customer Care Department within the U.S. at 800-956-7739, outside the U.S. at 317-572-3986, or fax 317-572-4002.

Jossey-Bass also publishes its books in a variety of electronic formats. Some content that appears in print may not be available in electronic books.

Library of Congress Cataloging-in-Publication Data

Bronfman, Charles.
  The art of giving : where the soul meets a business plan / Charles Bronfman, Jeffrey Solomon; foreword by James Wolfensohn.
    p. cm.
  Includes bibliographical references and index.
  ISBN 978-0-470-50146-7
1. Charities. 2. Nonprofit organizations—Management. I. Solomon, Jeffrey. II. Title.
HV40.B867 2009
361.7'6—dc22
                                    2009026352

Printed in the United States of America
FIRST EDITION
HB Printing   10 9 8 7 6 5 4 3 2 1

In memory of our parents:

Saidye and Sam

Herta and Martin

*whose values taught us to do our best in making
the world a better place.*

⁓

And in honor of our grandchildren:

Alexandra, Danielle, Lila, Lucy, Olivia, and Rainen

Samuel, Scott, Talia, and Zack

*who we know will continue the tradition to which
their parents are also committed.*

CONTENTS

FOREWORD

IF PHILANTHROPY IS THE LOVE OF MANKIND, then it is apt that this fine and helpful book should be dedicated to this subject, for it demonstrates its own love for humanity on every page. I do not mean love of the folksong variety that one sometimes encounters in charity work, but one that is more like tough love: it takes on the hard issues of a difficult trade in an unsentimental and clear-minded way, and it offers novel and compelling suggestions about ways that money, wisely applied, can make the world a better place. It is hard to imagine a potential donor who would not benefit from the insights of this book or to think of a veteran donor who won't wish that the book had been available sooner.

For all of its universality, to say nothing of its potency, philanthropy is little understood by the general public, or even by its practitioners. This book should go some way to change all that. And we owe a debt to Charles Bronfman and Jeffrey Solomon, who have been practitioners in the field for over a half-century between them, for setting down their ideas in such a fresh and readable fashion.

People who know nothing about philanthropy assume that it is easy. You reach into your wallet to pull out some cash for a small gift or write a check for a large one. Deliver the money to the recipient of your largess, and the work is done. Well, those of us who are in the business know that what has more likely just occurred is a waste of resources. Philanthropy cannot be so casual. It must be purposeful. It must connect.

Philanthropy involves both dreams and plans. You have to be inspired, and you have to be sensible. So many philanthropists miss this duality, erring too far in one direction or the other. But Bronfman and Solomon get it exactly right.

On the sensible side of the ledger, they are fierce advocates of measurement, a source of some controversy in the charitable community, which can be somewhat averse to hard numbers. As is often said, nonprofits have no bottom line, no easily recognizable and universally recognized measure of success. So they depend on other measures, often inconsistent and subjective, by which to determine when they are doing well and when they are doing badly. In insisting that nonprofits create and heed common measures of performance, Bronfman and Solomon are applying a welcome realism to a business sector that all too often lacks it completely.

The element of the book that is most inspiring is the one that is possibly the most daring: the authors' wise observation that philanthropy starts with you. Your feelings. Your dreams. Your values. And it makes you part of a broader world. By supporting causes outside your daily life, you not only do good for others, but you benefit by your involvement in the broader world in which we live. You learn about foreign lands, people of all types, and important causes, and you meet an extraordinary group of people. The act of giving is in fact a gift to oneself. Too many donors feel ashamed, or are made to feel ashamed, if they feel any personal gratification for the gifts they make. They are supposed to be selfless, a very odd notion if you think about it, as few people are on a regular basis. Just like any investor, donors are entitled to personal satisfaction for their financial contributions. And as Bronfman and Solomon point out, the pleasure that they take is their just reward for what they do, and it is also the source of their sustaining connection to the cause. It is what makes their work worth doing—for society and for them.

The big secret of philanthropy is now out. Philanthropy is fun. It is joyful. It is fulfilling. It will make your life feel worthwhile in ways that few other enterprises can.

Let this book show you how.

August 2009   James Wolfensohn
New York City

The Art
of Giving

INTRODUCTION

Who We Are

To many people, the world of nonprofits is like the dark side of the moon: mysterious, remote, and subject to unusual forces. We have spent a half-century working in this realm and hope this book will shed some light on the strange enterprise of doing good. We do this primarily for the sake of potential donors, who are, after all, essential to philanthropy. Without donors, there would be no philanthropy at all. No private universities, many fewer hospitals, no places of worship, precious few museums, and infinitely fewer programs for the poor, the arts, the elderly, the environment.

Despite their centrality, donors have few resources for solid information about making their gifts—deciding what the right gift is for them, how to structure it, how to consider the tax implications, and countless other complexities. And then there is the emotional aspect. Few donors are selfless, and that is fine. The question is, What self governs these philanthropic choices, or what portion of that self? Where does the donor's deep passion reside? What is he or she hoping to accomplish? Too often philanthropic gifts are made out of social or business obligation, guilt, or whim, which takes all the urgency and meaning out of them, to say nothing of the fun.

To give is a sweet verb. But it also runs counter to some basic human impulses—so counter, in fact, that we tend to think of the nonprofit world as the negative economy, an upside-down world where philanthropies are inverted versions of "actual" businesses or industries, spending money without making it. That mistaken idea leads to many others about the peculiar notion of existing to serve others and measuring success in terms other than dollars.

Such attitudes place philanthropy in a special preserve and require a special understanding. With this book, we're hoping to instruct donors, and would-be donors, on some of the truths of our trade, like the nature and definition of progress, the proper balance between ambition and resources, how to sort through the overwhelming number of opportunities, and such abstruse but essential matters as board governance and tax liabilities. Philanthropy can also be addictive. Where the donor's money goes, her heart is likely to follow.

We have divided this book into four parts to cover the essential elements that the donor needs to understand in order to make the most effective and satisfying gifts. Part One, "The Donor," is about just that: the donor herself. We situate her in the new philanthropic era, helping to identify her most authentic motivation, seeing where she fits within the wide range of donors, and guiding her as she selects the perfect gift to make. Of the three parts, it is the most psychological, since it necessarily delves into the soul where, we will argue, the essential motivations lie. This is not a book defining how you ought to do philanthropy. It is about discovering how you want to do philanthropy.

The parts that follow lay out the business plan that will turn the soulful aspirations of a potential donor into reality. Part Two, "The Partners," gets more practical. Philanthropy, after all, needs to be practical if it is going to succeed. The part proceeds from the assumption that few donors can go it alone, especially in a period of economic austerity. It lays out the connections a donor can make to maximize his impact on the world, whether it is working with a nonprofit agency to get the work done, coordinating with fellow board members to increase effectiveness, or establishing a family foundation that unites several generations in a common cause—and without the rancor that can attend such a venture. All of these strategies extend the donor's reach in the world, increase his leverage, and so boost impact.

And finally, in Part Three, "The Gift," we address the many complexities of the donation itself. Philanthropy is rarely as simple as writing a check, because it is important to recognize the legal, financial, tax, and practical implications of the various types of donation in order to identify the one or ones that work best for you. The best donors are the ones who are most knowledgeable and best prepared. To round out our donor's instruction, we lay out the many varieties of donation, ranging from the creation of complicated land trusts to the transfer of the rights to valuable intellectual property, and from the many attractions of unrestricted gifts to the surprising utility of event-related ones. We describe and evaluate the advantages and disadvantages of each. We also lay out our conviction that an essential element of philanthropy is measurement. If you can't measure the impact of your gift, you should not make it. Without measurement, there can be no confidence in success. For further assistance in this challenging realm, Part Four provides a broad range of more specialized resources.

And success is what we are committed to. In a realm of life that has no bottom line, no universally agreed-on definition of success, we offer this: success is accomplishing the objective that you set for your gift. If you give twenty-five thousand dollars to provide violins and instruction to fifty inner-city youths for three years, success is doing that. But we'd go further. Success is meeting an objective, yes, but success also means finding an objective that is worth achieving, given all the time, energy, and money it will require of you. Ultimately success is changing the world for the better. And the change begins with you. How do you want to change the world today?

—❧—

We're not experts, but we have been around. We have come to this calling by radically different routes. Charles Bronfman is the second son of Sam Bronfman, the storied founder of Seagram Company in Montreal. After dropping out of McGill University midway through his junior year to enter the family company, he was quickly put to work to learn all areas of the business: distilling and blending, accounts payable, sales and marketing.

After four years, Charles was put in charge of a smaller Canadian firm acquired by Seagram. Although it had several dozen salesmen across Canada, its domestic operations were poor. Charles turned it into a profitable business in a year. When he was twenty-five years old, Charles took over all of Seagram's marketing in Canada, and at age twenty-eight, he was appointed president of Seagram's Canadian operations. With increasing responsibilities through the years, he closed out his fifty-year career at the Seagram Company as its co-chairman.

Charles's father, Sam, became the leading Jewish philanthropist in Canada, giving time and money to many causes both within the Jewish and larger community, as he realized that any citizen of any country should give to the betterment of the country beyond his own group's interests. He delighted in the ways that philanthropy broadened his worldview.

Charles got involved at a young age, collecting fifty-cent pieces for the Montreal Jewish Appeal. "With responsibility must come authority" was his watchword. In his thirties, Charles became an officer of the Montreal Jewish Federation, the central planning, fundraising, and allocation organization in the Montreal Jewish community.

In 1968, Charles seized the opportunity to be founding owner of the Montreal Expos, the first of the Canadian expansion teams of Major League Baseball. It was a chance to shift from being an inheritor to being a pioneer. It also freed him from endless comparisons to his brother Edgar, who had emerged as the company head. With his new self-confidence, Charles decided to create the foundation that bears his name and that of his late wife, Andrea.

Through the Andrea and Charles Bronfman Philanthropies (ACBP), first in Montreal and now in New York City, he has maintained two overriding commitments. Charles has long been devoted to the cause of Israel, where he sponsors the largest educational enrichment program serving some 265,000 elementary school students annually. And through such programs as Birthright Israel, the ACBP aims to foster Jewish identity by sponsoring young people of Jewish descent on a free ten-day trip to Israel. As a native Canadian, Charles has also been distressed that his fellow Canadians have long defined themselves by what they are not. They are not Americans, not British, not French. The ACBP has backed an effort to define Canadians by what they are, primarily through a series of one-minute spots shown with the trailers in Canadian theaters extolling a variety of Canadian heroes in the Heritage Program. The ACBP now engages in $220 million worth of programmatic activities and has been hailed as a model foundation by the Philanthropy Roundtable. Charles and Andrea never imagined that the Philanthropies would continue indefinitely. Charles's two children were given adequate resources by their grandfather to continue their own philanthropy in their own way, so Charles and Andrea decided to have the ACBP spend down the foundation's corpus by 2016, when Charles turns eighty-five. In this way, the foundation can better concentrate on its mission and fulfill Charles's and Andrea's objectives. It also placed the emphasis on the work, not on the organization.

—☙

As the son of Jewish refugees from Germany, Jeffrey Solomon followed a different path to his life in philanthropy. His mother first worked in the United States as a housecleaner; his father was a butcher who ran a delicatessen in New York City's Gramercy Park. At the age of twelve, Jeff began working for his father stocking shelves, making sandwiches, and doing whatever else needed doing. The experience taught him a lesson he has carried through in non-profits: the work is never done. If there are customers, help them. If there aren't any customers, dust the shelves. If the shelves are dusted, slice the meat. From behind the counter, he also honed his people skills, engaging with everyone from the cops from the nearby police academy to the local businessmen, and even the occasional celebrity.

At a family deli, everyone does a bit of everything, and so Jeff learned the necessary skills of running a business—accounts payable, accounts receivable, inventory control—all of which proved useful training for handling the understaffed and overstrained nonprofits he would later run. He learned to look at the balance sheets of nonprofits and zero in on the bottom 10 percent that were headed for trouble rather than let his attention wander to the others that were doing fine. And he learned to ask the right questions.

Ultimately the deli business led directly to his nonprofit career. At that time, many of New York's social service agencies were located near Park Avenue South, just a couple of blocks from the store. Among his other duties, Jeff made deliveries, and in the process, he got to know many of the leaders in the field. When Jeff turned seventeen, one of them asked if he would like to pitch in at one of his agencies that summer. If it meant an end to delivering sandwiches, he would. So off he went to East Harlem and into the world of nonprofit agencies, with occasional detours into positions of government service.

Jeff's years in the family delicatessen were formative in terms of work ethic and business savvy, but he was also a product of his time. Entering the workforce in the 1960s, when most young people were questioning authority, helped make Jeff the new philanthropist he is today. From his earliest days in philanthropy, he had little patience for those many practices that were in place solely because they were in place. Also, in mental health, where he had done his early work, government money came to be increasingly influential, crowding out individual donations. And it made the arbitrary and self-serving ways of old philanthropy open to question too, which had decided rather whimsically who was eligible for the services of the program. As the government money came in, that became a matter for the professional staff, based on well-thought-out policy directives. That is to say, it started to be run like a business.

Jeff spent much of his early career in the social service and mental health fields in Miami and New York City and has also overseen this work in government at the city, state, and federal levels. A widely recognized authority on philanthropy, he was in charge of fundraising and grant making to over 120 agencies as the chief operating officer of UJA-Federation of New York before coming to the Charles and Andrea Bronfman Philanthropies as its president in 1997.

—❧

Together we would like to think we bring a fresh, enlivening approach to an enterprise that too often is undervalued and thought of as the province of the burned-out and overwhelmed. For the potential donor, volunteer, and even just the curious, we offer this book as a short course in how to be a street-smart, effective philanthropist regardless of your income level. We'll help you figure out your own relationship with charitable giving, sorting out what matters most to you and how to go about getting it. The world is filled with wonderful agencies with good intentions, but as you'll soon find, we are realists, and so we also will show you how to keep from getting picked clean by the vultures that circle this business — the supposedly disinterested philanthropic mentors who actually have only their own interests at heart. This is also a book for nonprofit program and development executives aiming at placing a donor-centered mirror up to their lives and their livings.

After so many decades of experience, we are not blind to the challenges of the field, but we are also alert to its excitement and promise. And we have a long history of turning that promise into product. Still, we have no investment in our way. We have an investment only in the best way. Philanthropic dollars are too precious, and the charitable needs are too great, for anyone to be satisfied with anything less.

PART ONE
The Donor

"I'M AFRAID I HAVE TO CLASSIFY YOU AS 'WEIRD', MR. HAINESWORTH. YOU JUST DON'T HAVE THE NET WORTH TO QUALIFY AS 'ECCENTRIC'."

Harvard Business Review, May–June 2000. Permission granted by Dave Carpenter.

CHAPTER 1

Getting Started

SAY YOU'RE SIXTY-SEVEN, AND YOU'VE SPENT your career turning your father's hardware store into a successful chain of stores throughout the Midwest, and you're ready for something else. Your children have no interest in taking over the business, so you decide to cash out. When the $50 million arrives by wire into your account, you are floating. Then it hits: What to do with so much money? You have vague thoughts of travel and a fondness for musical theater, but few interests beyond that. Your life has been your work. You're a widower, and you want to set some of the money aside for your children and to be comfortable yourself. But that still leaves well over $30 million. You're seized by the idea that you should be good to the society that has been so good to you. A major gift to your alma mater, perhaps, or possibly endowing a struggling theater in town? But, you wonder, aren't there more important causes? Wider-reaching ones perhaps? Ones where you could get involved yourself?

But what?

Or maybe you're forty-three, with a fistful of stock options in a company that was nothing more than a bunch of interesting algorithms when you first signed on and now has grown to dominate the market for software that assists in securing online purchases. The options have skyrocketed in value nearly a thousand-fold, making your net worth jump from about $17,000, or whatever your car and clothes were worth at the age of twenty-four when you joined the company, to somewhere north of $10 million today. You're unmarried, with just a cat for regular company—and you aren't the type to give everything to her. You have your own financial security to consider. But that still leaves at least $5 million "extra," as you think of it. And with everything that is going on in the world, you feel a little weird about having so much money just sitting in your investment account. You've contributed to political campaigns, donated a few thousand dollars to breast cancer research and other causes, but now you're thinking that maybe you should do more to make a positive difference in the world.

But what?

Or perhaps you're thirty-nine and you certainly aren't rich, but you do make a decent income, and you'd like to give some of it away. You don't have enough to end hunger in sub-Saharan Africa, but you are hoping to do a little good in a world that so plainly needs it. Plus, you like the idea of being connected to a cause that is larger than yourself. You give regularly to your local NPR station and have faithfully contributed to your college's alumni fund, although you sometimes wonder why. But now you're thinking that you'd like to bundle the money you make available for those gifts, and maybe add a little more, to come up with a few thousand dollars a year that might really help one cause—and be more satisfying for you too. But you look around, and all you can think is that everywhere you look is need. Still, you definitely want to do something.

But what?

Or let's say you're twenty-five. You've been at your first job for a few years now and recently got a raise with your first promotion. You rent, have a roommate, and tend to be economical. So even after your student loans and car payments, you have a bit left over. You see what is going on in the world, and you'd like to do something to help. Your company will match your donations dollar for dollar. But there are so many choices! You're besieged by requests from friends to sponsor them on charitable walks, runs, rides, events. And that's nothing compared to all the appeals that come in the mail or from homeless people on the street. And you have your own organizations and causes you would like to support. You don't have that much money, but you would like to do something smart and useful with it.

But what?

—☙—

If you see yourself in one of these vignettes, you are not alone. There are millions of people like you—well-meaning people who have more money than they need, would like to do something worthwhile with it, and are baffled as to what. It is not for lack of funds. In the first half of this century, before the downturn of 2008 skewed projections, it was predicted that $40 trillion would be passed down to the baby boomers from their parents and grandparents of the World War II generation. $40 trillion: that's four hundred times this year's military budget, twelve times the entire outlay of the federal government, and three times the nation's gross domestic product. It was enough to create 40 million millionaires. And this is not including the wealth created more recently by hedge fund managers, venture capitalists, real estate developers, founders of computer and Internet companies, and other holders of equity stakes in growing businesses—all of whom have come into tremendous fortunes seemingly overnight.

Although the full impact of the recent economic downturn is not yet known, our faith in American resilience leads us to believe that while the numbers may change, the issue will again emerge. But all the more striking are the donors who are not rich but are hard working, who, for all the emphasis on the Gateses of the world, constitute the bulk of the donors in the new philanthropy. Of

2007's record-breaking $306.39 billion in charitable contributions, individuals contributed 74.8 percent, the majority of the givers having incomes under $100,000. (Corporations, foundations, and bequests accounted for the rest.) The prewar generation was more generous than the baby boomers, who were in turn more generous than Generation X, but mostly that is because disposable income is a function of age, and giving increases with income. Some of the money comes out of salaries, the rest from wise investments in real estate or the stock market. Whatever the source, the full array of such wealth is potentially the single greatest source for good in American history and, arguably, in the history of all mankind. Even as we adjust to lowered expectations, philanthropy will grow relative to other components of the economy.

As Tocqueville first pointed out, of all nationalities, Americans have the most fervid volunteer spirit, stemming from a conviction that the people should retain a greater power than the government to transform society. And so, to the astonishment of foreigners, America is the land of nonprofits. From universities to hospitals, from arts associations to day care centers, nonprofits are a tremendous part of this nation's gross national product. If the nonprofit sector were a single industry, it would be by far the largest industry in the United States, employing one out of every ten American workers.

So as a donor, can you just sprinkle your money over a few congenial nonprofits with nice brochures and celebrity endorsements, and then watch these institutions crank out good works? Perhaps. But for all of its many assets, the nonprofit sector, like all others, is pockmarked with tragically underperforming elements. Just as there are killer stocks and there are duds, the investor in nonprofits faces a welter of good, not-so-good, and third-rate organizations clamoring for his money. Which ones are which? We certainly can't evaluate them all. Those that have (such as Charity Navigator) look at financial efficiency due to the challenges of sectorwide performance measurements of effectiveness and value. We think of philanthropy in investment terms—investments for a better world. Although, as we will point out, the challenge in nonprofits is often choosing between good and good, there are enough underperforming ones that donors should be wary. Too many nonprofits lack clear purpose, effective leadership, and competent management, and their highest priority appears to be preserving their own existence. We assail these underperformers because such entities turn the spiritual act of giving into a frustrating game.

It is important to remember that a nonprofit is a business, and it should be run as one, with no less an emphasis on efficiency, transparency, and accountability than you would find in its for-profit counterparts—indeed, more so. Although we celebrate the differences between mission-oriented nonprofits and profit-oriented businesses, we acknowledge the gap in measurements, benchmarks, and markets. The economic meltdown that began in late 2008 underscores the fallibility of unabashed business modeling. Nevertheless, the principles and experience of transparent competition can serve societal needs beyond the simple marketplace.

Charity Versus Philanthropy

Philanthropy is hard to do well. It is far more difficult to design and run a nonprofit than it is to manage a for-profit company of equivalent size. Why? Because in the nonprofit world, there is no

15

single, universally agreed-on measure of success. Now we believe in measures, and work very hard to create them, and we use them to evaluate our own endeavors. But it is not obvious what those measures are, for there is no built-in bottom line of profit and loss of return on investment. Without such measures, nonprofits too often are flying blind, relying on guesswork as to where they are and where they are headed. And those guesses can be way off.

Plus, nonprofits are being buffeted about by enormous changes in the world of philanthropy, not the least of them stemming from the baby boomers' new approach to giving. Their parents largely believed in funding umbrella institutions like the United Way and Catholic Charities, which decided for them how the funds were to be spent. This was that generation's idea of saluting society for the benefits it had received. The baby boomers, by contrast, believe in making a difference personally. They want to choose for themselves the recipients of their donation and monitor the effects. Their parents usually called their giving "charity." The boomers prefer to call theirs "philanthropy."

There is a plethora of nonprofits in the United States, over 1.7 million in all, and they are often staffed by untrained volunteers who can be difficult to manage without financial inducements. The talent pool for paid management staff is shallow. Who do you know who made it his life's ambition to run a nonprofit? Not too many people, most likely. Compared to for-profit equivalents, the salaries are paltry, the status not much better, and precious few university programs offer these professionals any serious instruction. And the objectives are daunting: curing Alzheimer's disease, feeding the poor in Africa, developing new models for elementary school education.

Now into this jumble comes you, the neophyte donor, eager to make a difference with your money. Most likely, you have no direct experience with nonprofits beyond having been a consumer of some nonprofit service in a hospital or school, or done some volunteer work, or perhaps served on a board. Typically you have given the topic a fraction of the attention that you have lavished on your career, family, social life, hobbies, or investments. And yet you expect to engage in serious philanthropy before the week is out.

If it were that easy, those of us who have made philanthropy our life's work would have written novels, or composed symphonies, or engaged in many other extracurricular activities in our copious free time. Truth is, philanthropy makes serious demands not only on your pocketbook but also on your intellect, feelings, attention, and time. Nothing of value comes for free. If you are willing to give fully of yourself, you will receive satisfactions that are hard to come by on the for-profit side: the thrill of seeing your idea sent forth into the world to improve countless other people's lives. It's the joy of connection, of enlarging yourself. Yes, there truly is a joy to giving.

Philanthropy as we practice it shares one of the major principles of the for-profit world, and that is accountability. In some respects, old school charity was quick and easy in that it freed donors from significant social obligation. Donors could give a few hundred dollars to the United Way or place a few bills in the plate at church without having any particular idea where that money was going, who decided, why, and what good, if any, came of it. The institutions were unassailable repositories of probity and good sense. They knew better than anyone else how to fix any ills that beset society.

It's unclear how many people ever believed that, but few believe it now. Most people, quite rightly, believe that they are entitled to follow their money and see what it does, and if it's nothing, to look elsewhere for a nonprofit investment. Nowadays a donor can rightly expect that the nonprofit will make the most of his gift by leveraging it to the hilt. And he should feel free to ask tough questions when it fails to. This new business-mindedness is the norm. Nonprofits should be run just as crisply as for-profits. Meetings should start on time and end on time too. They should not be social gatherings that drag on endlessly for no purpose. A nonprofit isn't church either. It should not fall for a charismatic leader who gives the operation a charged-up, religious feeling—and loses sight of what it is actually created to do.

It's All About You

You have every right to insist on best practices in any organization you are going to favor with a donation, but you also need to focus on yourself. This may seem antithetical in an area of life that seems to rely on the most abject sort of selflessness: giving your hard-earned money to benefit people you don't know. But every transaction is an exchange; nothing is ever one way. When you give, you get, and we believe you need to focus on what it is that you are getting for what you give. We argue that what you get in philanthropy is nourishment for that portion of the body that is so sacred it cannot be found in any book of anatomy: the soul, where all that is best in us resides. It is simultaneously the innermost self and the one so external it seems somehow eternal—which makes it the natural connection point for our philanthropy, for we give to improve the world in a lasting way and to leave it with our stamp.

CHAPTER 2

The Joy of Giving

JOY. THAT IS A CENTRAL CHARACTERISTIC of the nonprofit world, or it should be. Philanthropy is a matter of giving—of yourself as much as of your money. And the more you give, the more you stand to get back—not in money, obviously, but in more spiritual forms of value. Connection. Purpose. Meaning. All the elements that people seek in a paying job but rarely find. Think of the greatest secular saints of our day: Albert Schweitzer, Mother Teresa, Paul Farmer. All of them radiated optimism, hope, energy. Their humble, and sometimes desperate, surroundings did not bring them down but charged them up.

What makes philanthropy so satisfying? Consider the square in Figure 2.1 with the four most significant social forces marked on the corners: religion, government, family, and economy. Each is largely confined to its own corner. As the illustration shows, there is only one element of social life that catches up all four and fills in the gaps between them. Philanthropy. It has some of the spiritual quality of religion; it derives from the economy; it complements the work of government; and it extends the sense of family. Connecting these separate quadrants of our lives, philanthropy can act as an integrating force that is fulfilling precisely because it is so full of such diverse, and yet essential, elements.

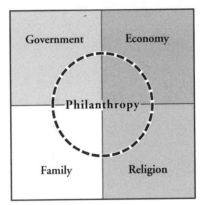

Figure 2.1. **The Four Corners of the Public Square**

Acting with Intentionality

Another satisfaction in philanthropy is expressed by a word that you don't hear very much but means a lot to us. *Intentionality*. It's the art of doing things purposefully. Because philanthropy involves a decision between right and right, to many people the choice hinges on a fairly slight difference, such as whether a close friend or a not-so-close friend asked them to, or whether "everybody" was doing it. But there's a higher stage of involvement, and that is doing something in philanthropy because they themselves really want to do it. The mission is their mission. They believe in it. It matters. It reaches to the deepest part of them.

There are any number of ways to express that, but we liken it to the purchase of art. We should first say that we have a lot of art on display at the Andrea and Charles Bronfman Philanthropies (ACBP) foundation, most of it by Canadian artists. The works were not particularly expensive or the artists well known. But the pieces are all lively and colorful, and they lift the spirits of everyone who sees them. And that was the idea.

Charles and his late wife, Andrea, brought something wonderful out of the nothing that was the vacant corners and empty walls that stood in the office before. By bringing this art to the space, they created a cheerful, uplifting, enlivening environment that had not existed before. We like to think that all of philanthropy holds that possibility.

Intentionality is a special characteristic of the new philanthropy, which is far more considered than the old. Typically the old philanthropy was a matter of fulfilling an obligation: you gave the same amount to the same cause, year after year, as regular as taxes, which the payments somewhat resembled. With the best of the new philanthropy, donors make gifts that are meaningful to them, that connect at a deep level.

It can be an effort, though. So much in our lives as consumers is a matter of making a choice between A and B. Do we want to fly to Rio de Janeiro on February 1 at 11:15 A.M. on an American Airlines flight with two stops for $823, or leave at 1:25 P.M. on a U.S. Airways flight with one stop for $975? Choices like that don't exist in philanthropy. They don't match up on the same metric. Instead, you have to decide for yourself what you want out of it. This is being intentional.

Do you get a hundred dollars' worth of services for a contribution of a hundred dollars? The truth is, you can't know. The fear is that you may get less. But precisely because philanthropy is not monetized, its yield can be all the greater, generating a value that goes beyond money altogether, if you act with intentionality and aim to secure the gratification you seek.

Look again at that square in Figure 2.1, and consider what the elements at each corner actually do. The economy is all about transactions—the purchase and sale of goods and services. The government provides military security and social infrastructure for its citizens. The family is for raising children and transmitting values. And religion is the source of many of those values. Viewed this way, the four elements are more self-contained, and they leave all the more room for philanthropy to expand into them. To be sure, philanthropy is never disinterested. You give money to your alma mater because you are grateful for the superior education and the financial aid you received that permitted you to take advantage of that opportunity. You can put a dollar value on your gift, but its greatest value lies in the way it evokes the four elements. It has the spirit of religion, the bond of family, the urgency of an economic force, and the power of government. It is an act of love that goes from you, through others, and out into the world to produce a needed change. You know that others will experience in the future that same opportunity that served you so well in the past. This is the joy of giving.

CHAPTER 3

The New Philanthropy

PAUL SCHERVISH OF BOSTON COLLEGE, possibly the foremost researcher on philanthropic motivations, reports that donors used to support nonprofits to help them achieve their mission. Now we support nonprofits so that they can help *us* achieve *our* personal mission. In the realm of nonprofits, it's a transformation as dramatic as the one that Copernicus created in society when he discovered that the sun did not revolve around the earth, but the reverse.

The legendary General Electric CEO Jack Welch once remarked that the problem with the world is that people want to take their second bow when the world is waiting for a second act. For a long time, philanthropy was all about the second bow—an opportunity for accomplished people to receive another round of acclaim for giving away the money they had already been honored for making. In that scheme, philanthropy was about power, expectation, influence, and, yes, ego. It was rarely about impact.

Until now. In the new philanthropy, donors have sought to make a difference. They are ready for their second act. And they are ready to make use of the sophisticated management instruments they have developed in their business life to achieve greater performance in this new, more challenging arena, and with potentially more impact. They give purposefully, think strategically, rely on measurements and regular monitoring. In short, they are relying on the focus and rigor of for-profit businesses to enhance the effectiveness of their philanthropy. We know that business is far from perfect. It can be misguided and inefficient, and many of its most promising enterprises can fail. Moreover, the marketing of goods and services for the best competitive price is no model for philanthropy. However, its best attributes of purposeful, honed intelligence and strategic-mindedness have a place in philanthropy, and we should be hospitable to them in the nonprofit world and celebrate their use.

In the old philanthropy, giving was often defensive. Earlier donors gave largely out of obligation, routine, and guilt, if not to gain influence, social standing, or a place in heaven. They gave, in short, largely because they had to. Not so with the new philanthropists. They have something completely different in mind, something far more assertively positive. The successful entrepreneurs of the dot-com world are the ones generally credited with the creation of the new philanthropy, and they remain the model of the new philanthropist. They made their money earlier in their lives than the most prominent donors of previous generations, who followed after Rockefeller and Carnegie in regarding philanthropy as the culmination of a long and prosperous business career. And unlike their predecessors, they brought to the philanthropic sector some of the élan of their for-profit careers, as well as a nearly theological belief in a close connection to their customers and a quasi-scientific monitoring of results. Curiously, another source of such an approach is much less well known. It is in the distinctive philanthropy of socially minded women. For them, philanthropy was rarely the check-signing exercise that it was for men. Since so many women were excluded from the workforce, they tended to have a different relationship to money than men did. Women tended to be more diligent than men about identifying goals and objectives, determining an approach, and measuring impact.

In the new philanthropy, the donors' giving is like their doing: it is individual, forward looking, leveraged for effect, and bent on changing the world. The old philanthropy has certainly not disappeared. The United Way, the great emblem of the old philanthropy, is still the largest charity in the United States. (The second largest is the Salvation Army.) But the new philanthropy has an influence that goes far beyond its monetary value, for it signifies the transformation of society from a standard of noblesse oblige to one of entrepreneurial problem solving and, ultimately, of success.

The new philanthropist looks at her activities with a refreshing frankness and realism. She is less saint than engineer. She has two essential questions that she asks herself and others in the organization every day: What are my goals? How do I define success? When the Robin Hood Foundation began its work, led by several visionary hedge fund players, they set a clear if wildly ambitious goal: to eradicate poverty in New York. That purpose dictated every tactical decision they subsequently made. Run programs or fund programs? Use community-based organizations or larger nonprofits? Simply make grants or be venture capitalists? How to measure progress? How long to allow? What infrastructural support would be required? What kind of a board? A blizzard of questions, but it was met by a blizzard of answers. Knowing the objective made it possible to obtain the result.

It will not be a surprise that the median age of the principals of the Robin Hood Foundation is considerably lower than that in your father's charities. It takes a young person to have such energizing hubris, if not the outright gall, to think that poverty can be ended in New York City or anywhere else. But youth provides much of the energy of the new philanthropy—not only young people, but old people who act like young people.

Never before have young people had such a role in phi-lanthropy. But as the younger generation, and still younger generations, have come of age, philanthropy has spread across the life span in new and exciting ways. Right now, for the first time in history, four generations sit at the same nonprofit workbench, each with a unique worldview based on the historical moment that shaped it. In considering the new philanthropy, it is important to understand these four generations, their distinctions and overlaps, for the intergenerational dynamic establishes much of the unique character of the new philanthropy. Yes, it is very much colored by the rising generations, but it is also shaped by its resistance to some of the older ways of being. So let us delineate them here:

—☙

- *Traditionals.* These came of age during World War II, many of them serving in the military and earning them the title of Greatest Generation. Born between 1925 and 1945, many of them experienced the Great Depression and forever after have saved for a rainy day. By disposition, they are respectful of authority and institutions and expect to be treated with similar respect themselves. Because they preceded the media inundation that has shaped the attitudes and consciousness of their descendants, their children and grandchildren often have trouble communicating with these stalwarts of a bygone era.
- *Baby boomers.* The generation born after World War II, the largest cohort of the four, was the nation's primary social, media, economic, and advertising focus—until Generation Y (the "echo boom") arrived. While the boomers' outlook has been shaped by network TV, which grew up with them, their politics have largely been derived, pro or con, from the rebellions of the 1960s. From civil rights to women's rights to antiwar movements, the boomers learned advocacy and

leadership early on. As the oldest ones now straddle sixty-four years old, they are confronting the reality of giving up control to their Gen X children or finding their next leadership opportunity.

- *Generation X.* Born amid Iran-Contra, Watergate, and the downsizing of corporations their parents worked for for decades, Gen Xers are cynical about government and the market. As they grew, they were confronted with the AIDS epidemic, the Gulf War, and the bubble boom and bust of the 1990s dot-coms. These ups and downs, however, make Gen X a resilient, resourceful, and independent cohort eager to bring their creativity and skills to the table.

- *Generation Y.* Born between 1980 and 2000, Gen Y experienced Oklahoma City, Columbine, Hurricanes Katrina and Rita, 9/11, and Iraq, harkening back to the turmoil of the traditionals' era scores before. Given these events, they are more inclined to vote and volunteer than Gen X, and their spirit is fueled by the exponential growth in technology this cohort has been raised on. The Internet, text messaging, IM'ing, Twittering, and Facebook have brought them social connectivity and access to networks and causes, leaving them speaking a virtually different language from their parents and grandparents.

_⌒☡_

Distrustful of authority, frustrated with institutions, impatient for change, and embracing the new technologies: these are some of the philosophical underpinnings of the new philanthropy as it pulls away from the attitudes of the traditionals and pushes ahead to move toward the beliefs of Generation Y. The new philanthropy is, in this way, ever new.

Philanthropy is in the business of change. Like waves on the beach, one generation rises up, only to crest and subside as it reaches the shore, and then the one behind it does the same, and so on back through the generations. But the changing generations reflect a changing society. Indeed, they are the cause of that changing society. And it is important for philanthropists both new and old to recognize the relentlessness of the change that we all participate in. One of the things the philanthropist needs to discern is who is for change and who is against it. As we said in the 1960s, if you're not part of the solution, you're part of the problem. Change requires fluidity and rejects rigidity.

Yes, the new philanthropy embraces business principles, but it does so only to achieve a greater good. If it doesn't achieve that, we say revise it. The new philanthropy is not so much about process as it is about outcomes, about making change happen, about success. And that, in the end, is the soul of the new philanthropy.

CHAPTER 4

Donors Come
in All Types

A DONOR'S GIFT IS A UNIQUE EXPRESSION, almost as if it is a creative act. Yet just as painters fall into broad classifications—by historical period, say, or preferred medium—donors too can be classified by style and type. The essential distinction is between active and passive, although this is something of a misnomer since both categories of donor are fully engaged in the enterprise. The passive donor, however, gives only his money and leaves it at that. The active one uses his money to push the organization to better achieve its mission. The categories often overlap within each of us and should not be seen as mutually exclusive. They do, however, encourage the intentionality that is central to successful philanthropy.

The Nondonor

There is an important player here who is neither active nor passive, and probably shouldn't be included at all, except for the fact that he is a near-total preoccupation of the nation's nonprofits. We are speaking of the nondonor, who makes up about 30 percent of the American public. Yes, him, the one who is approached time and again with pitches for one worthy cause or another, only to turn them all down flat. And he is not necessarily being churlish. Let's face it: money is tight. Groceries and heat and tuition come first. And many nondonors feel that it is enough of a charitable contribution just to pay their taxes.

In this book, we do not intend to assert any sort of hierarchy of good, by which those who contribute more are morally superior to those who contribute less, and all are superior to those who contribute nothing. We're just describing the donor world as it is, with no claims about how it should be.

The nondonor represents a powerful impulse in the nonprofit world, one who shapes it, probably, more than any other. There is nothing quite like the word *no* to inspire nonprofits to get potential donors to *yes*.

And we should add that there is another kind of nondonor. She never contributes money, but she does contribute her time as she helps out at the PTA or runs a bake sale or coaches Little League or does so many of the other tasks that keep alive the organizations that hold communities together.

The Passive Donor

The passive donor exists at all socioeconomic levels, from the college student who kicks in twenty-five dollars to the local PBS affiliate, on up to the software engineer who gives $10 million, no strings attached, to his alma mater. This is solely a matter of writing a check. When the check is safely in the mailbox or the computer mouse is clicked, the philanthropic engagement is complete. This donor is passive in the sense that he is most likely responding to an appeal. He is not seeking an opportunity or following through with his own volunteer efforts.

The Reluctant Donor

This refers to the class of donor who is a nondonor in all but name but who nonetheless maintains a loyalty that can be tapped into by a particular cause. The reluctant donor makes no year-end gifts, serves on no boards, and views the IRS, begrudgingly, as his only charitable cause. He has many good reasons not to give, even when he has the money. The morning newspaper provides them every day. The outrageous salaries of senior executives! The ridiculous overhead! The wasteful services to offensive and unworthy recipients! And, besides, everyone knows that philanthropy is all about ego!

Strongly as he may feel about them, all these reasons fade into pale excuses when two of his best friends take him to lunch at an elegant restaurant and put the arm on him. They tell him about an immensely worthy cause in their home town and how each of them has already made a substantial pledge, and, well, surely he wouldn't want to be known as the only one who failed to come through. Thus a nondonor becomes a donor.

We certainly understand the resistance. The nonprofit side of the ledger is inherently dubious, at least as compared to the for-profit side. If you order a 42-inch flat-screen TV from Best Buy for delivery at your home, you have a reasonable confidence that the TV will be ready for viewing in your living room before too long. And if it isn't, you have recourse. But if you give five hundred dollars to the American Red Cross to help the victims of Hurricane Katrina, you don't have any assurances whatsoever that *your* five hundred dollars will actually benefit Katrina victims at all. And given the scandals that occasionally surface in the philanthropic world, it might not. That is to say, in the for-profit world, five hundred dollars generally buys five hundred dollars worth of goods or services. In nonprofits, five hundred dollars buys—well, who knows exactly. If you're a reluctant donor, you want guarantees

31

that your money will do what's claimed. Nonprofits don't give guarantees. You have to take their claims on faith. For this reason, the reluctant donor is likely to remain reluctant.

The Social Donor

The social donor gives generously to support her community, usually by heading or attending charity-driven events—everything from elegant balls to Las Vegas nights. On the upscale end of things, Palm Beach is a classic example of a community dominated by social donors. Nobody goes anywhere in Palm Beach after 6:00 P.M. except to benefit some cause, be it the local Leukemia Society or the Norton Museum. For the social donor, charity is the route to society, a way of freeing herself from some of the guilt that might otherwise adhere to a fancy dinner that was just that. It is also a way to create a cozy community of similar folks. For the social donor, a gift is equally a fiscal and a social act.

The Casual Donor

Then there's the casual donor. *Casual* doesn't mean slight. The gifts can be substantial, but as a rule, they are not particularly well considered. More serious donors consider overall strategy, relationship building, and personal history. Not so the casual donor. She scarcely thinks about philanthropy at all. Toward the end of the year, largely for tax purposes, she starts writing checks in response to whatever appeals she's received in the past few weeks and keeps writing until she's tired of it or reached a threshold. The levels of gift are a little arbitrary too. Five hundred for this, twenty-five hundred for that, seventy-five for this other one—even twenty-five-dollar gifts, which probably cost at least that much for the nonprofit to process. The randomness cedes much of the control to the solicitors and whatever strategy they can develop to lure donors into their pitch and write that check.

The Self-Promoting Donor

While it may sound antithetical to the whole philanthropic enterprise, self-promotion is actually a fairly common feature. A certain type of donor evaluates all of his potential giving on one basis: What's in it for him? How will it advance his agenda? His social standing? Will it bring him new business? Will it put his name in the paper or in lights? Philanthropy is not for saints, so it should not be shocking that some people want to get a personal return on their donation. All acts are selfish to some degree, or we would not do them. Although philanthropy is a gift, not a purchase, it is a nearly universal impulse to trade a quid for a quo. The person who "selflessly" chairs the United Way campaign is also the one who makes sure her name is prominent on the campaign letterhead. To which we say, fine. For the self-promoter, however, the contribution of his time is the good part. This is where he gets to show himself off. In a way, he pays for that privilege, and the money he gives is payment for the time he can put himself on display.

Again, we do not intend to deride this. It is all a reasonable calculation, and society is the beneficiary. The nonprofit world would have many fewer buildings, wings, entrances, and staircases if they did not offer naming opportunities in exchange for a donation. This is self-promoting, sure, but it is self-promoting in a good cause. As far as we are concerned, anything that advances that cause is all to the good. All of philanthropy is a branding,

33

or rebranding, opportunity, as countless movie stars in need of an identity makeover have discovered, and it is a chance for the donor to buff his own image through the act. It can be helpful to the donor, and to the recipient, to recognize such a significant aspect of his gift.

The Perils of Self-Promoting Philanthropy

Back in 1997, the *New York Times* reported on a small war that broke out over naming rights at the Central Park Zoo. A well-known philanthropic couple planned to give the zoo $3 million, and the zoo would rename the lovely petting zoo in their honor. The name would appear on a plaque by the entrance. But, the story goes, the donors were outraged to discover that the zoo would limit the height of their names on the sign to two inches.

While things smoldered, the zoo found an alternative approach. The would-be donors had been in a public dispute regarding values and philanthropy with another leading family. After the donors withdrew their offer to the zoo, the other family agreed to give $4.5 million and accepted the two-inch height restriction on the commemorative sign.

The Kennedy School at Harvard University now uses this as a philanthropic case study, sounding a cautionary note on the perils of donors going so public with their desires for acknowledgment. Fame can quickly turn to notoriety. Still, often lost in this tale of gossip and vengeance is the fact that both families are among New York's most generous donors to important causes.

The Strategic Donor

Unlike the self-promoting donor, the strategic donor is nearly selfless: she is using her philanthropic dollars primarily to advance an important cause, and without regard to how it affects her personally. Altruism for her is indeed an overriding motive. This donor starts by deciding what she wants to accomplish and then determines how to make it happen through philanthropy. Often these are big goals, such as turning a life-threatening disease like leukemia into a chronic one. Their very audacity dictates the need for strategizing; these goals will not be met easily. The strategic donor has to be versatile, since there is not necessarily a single path to success. And so it may very well be that money alone is not enough, that the goal will require a lot more of her than just her wallet. She will likely have to put in time to recruit others, to chart the course, perhaps even create a superstructure for making change happen.

The Social Entrepreneur

As the name suggests, the social entrepreneur is usually the creator of her favorite charity, much as the for-profit entrepreneur is the founder of her business. Like the strategic donor, the social entrepreneur does not contribute just money. To say she is giving her time is an understatement too, for she is really giving her energy, enthusiasm, creativity, passion, connections—everything that she's got to be a powerful force for change. And social entrepreneurs are everywhere. One stands behind every one of the 1.7 million nonprofits in the country.

She can be a marvel, a delight, a thrill. But she can also be, shall we say, difficult. The operation is her baby, and there can be

35

an "I, me, mine" mentality. On the for-profit side, this is called founder's syndrome, and it is an understandable consequence of the huge personal investment a company's creator has put in. But it can also breed a disposition by which the founder knows best, and no one else's opinion is given much time. Often the passion is understandable. The founders of a particular nonprofit have acted out of a fierce determination borne of a particularly compelling set of circumstances. They are parents, let's say, of a developmentally disabled son, and they are determined to create a playground that is suited to his needs. But what about all the other kids with that disability? Shouldn't the parents advocate for them too? Along with the tax deduction comes a responsibility to serve a wider clientele. Most social entrepreneurs learn to adapt as they learn about the extent of need, and their organizations are the better for it.

Even with her liabilities, the social entrepreneur still represents the best of the new philanthropy, which is all about importing the best of the for-profit world and putting it to use on the nonprofit side. If the old philanthropy was about entrenched and somewhat stuck charitable institutions, the new philanthropy is about nimble, market-focused, high-leverage agencies with a big impact that kill themselves to deliver change. And the energy behind them is the passion of the social entrepreneur, who likely put her life on hold to make this happen. To our way of thinking, the social entrepreneur is a great American hero.

─◌─

Just because there are many types of donor doesn't mean you fit into just one of them any more than you can be characterized by just one aspect of your personality. A donor might be reluctant to give to the hospital but generous to the symphony, serving on its board as well as writing large checks annually. So much of philanthropy is—and should be—personal. You care about this and not so much about that, and not at all about some third thing. Such flexibility shows your individuality—and your intentionality.

A Better Way

There are thousands of social entrepreneurs in the country today, but one of the more innovative is a real estate professional named Ron Bruder. His eldest daughter worked in the World Trade Center area, and he was so distressed at the thought that she might have been killed in the September 11 attacks that he vowed he would do whatever he could to keep such a catastrophe from ever happening again. But how? He decided that the key factor in the 9/11 attack was the lack of economic opportunity and high unemployment that exists in many countries in the Middle East, specifically affecting young men. So he resolved to try to make the economies of the Middle Eastern countries more hospitable to young men, with an eye toward giving them the possibility of meaningful employment and a greater stake in life than the radical Islam being preached in certain parts of the world. He started the Education for Employment Foundation, which fosters radically increasing employment prospects for young men and women through innovative, educational programs. It has now grown to five countries across the Middle East: Jordan, Egypt, Morocco, West Bank/Gaza, and Yemen.

CHAPTER 5

The Soul of the New Philanthropist

GIVEN THE UNIVERSE OF NEED, HOW CAN a single donor make a significant difference? It is tempting to think of philanthropy as a kind of consumer purchase, buying a little less hunger, or a little more literacy, with each check or click of a mouse. But serious philanthropy is serious work, and like all other work, it requires a fair amount of preparation, skill, insight, and diligence.

In their careers, after all, most people train for decades, gradually working their way up from the bottom, before they find the job that really suits them. It is one of the liabilities of philanthropy that there isn't a similar development process for donors. Worse, donors tend to assume that their business experience immediately converts to philanthropic acumen. But it doesn't. Philanthropy is in a realm of its own.

It is for this reason that the most successful donors don't just plunge right into their philanthropy. They go in slowly, and it can take a while to get acclimated. Just to decide what they want to do can take a while. Bill Gates thought about his philanthropy for years before deciding to get into the work of combating infectious diseases in Africa, and Andrew Carnegie did the same before determining that he wanted to create a national network of public libraries. Precious few significant acts of philanthropy are spontaneous.

At the Andrea and Charles Bronfman Philanthropies, we do not believe in steering people while they formulate their choices, but we have often sat down with potential donors to help them come up with an approach to giving that feels right to them. As we like to say, philanthropy isn't a matter of just doing the right thing; it is a matter of doing the right thing for you. If your heart isn't in it, you're likely to get bored, distracted, and listless, and your philanthropic enterprise will end up in the doldrums. So a large part of our effort is to try to help them find the course that moves them most.

How? By looking within. By delving into their soul. Yes, that word again, but there really is no other. Successful philanthropy comes from a deep place in the human psyche. It's about finding yourself in this work, sure. But it is also about love. Philanthropy is all about love—literally. The word means "love of humankind." But what does that mean? Which aspect of humankind? This is what Jeff tries to help each donor discover for himself.

Talking the Talk

From his background in the mental health field, Jeff has a clinical orientation and is usually the one to work with donors to help them sort their dreams and desires to decide on their philanthropic missions. It isn't therapy, he would like to emphasize, but it is serious, probing, intimate conversation to gain access to the core motivations that define people.

To this example, Jeff is working with Marge, a well-educated, middle-aged woman. She seems edgy as they sit together in his office, and she tells him that after her divorce a few years back, she received several million dollars in a settlement. She'd like to devote a fair percentage of it to philanthropy. Coming to her the way it did, the money doesn't feel as if it is really hers.

In such conversations, Jeff starts out gently, so he begins by asking Marge about her previous experience with philanthropy. What has she been giving to already? Her college? The Red Cross? The local hospital?

"To Smith, modestly," she says shyly. "And to the Audubon Society. Just a few hundred dollars."

These answers can be guides to her interests right there. To determine their depth and solidity, Jeff probes further: Which of these gifts gives her the greater satisfaction? (Shrug.) How about her parents? What have they been giving to?

"Their church, primarily. Presbyterian."

Is that a cause that she'd like to continue to support?

Marge shakes her head.

Or, going further back, are there any "heritage" gifts—ones that stem from a tradition of family giving? To the United Way or Salvation Army maybe?

"Just the church," Marge repeats.

Such gifts can establish useful guidelines. Here past performance can indeed indicate future results. It can also be reassuring for Marge to realize that she is not coming into this new business totally cold. She has confronted these choices before, and made them, choosing causes that were of personal interest to her and different from those of her parents.

Then Jeff goes deeper, reaching for those moments of unexpectedly heavy emotion that people tend to set aside as momentary lapses, but that he finds to be revealing of a more fundamental mind-set. Tears are especially significant. They mark the path to where the deepest feelings lie. He asks Marge when she last choked up at the movies, and what moved her.

"Maybe it was *E.T.,* when the little extraterrestrial phones home?" Jeff nudged. "Or the movie *Finding Neverland,* when the J. M. Barrie character falls in love with Kate Winslet and her four boys?"

The important thing isn't the movie, but the donor's reaction to it. The precise nature of the connection can be very revealing, for people don't feel for the character nearly so much as they feel for themselves. If it's *Saving Private Ryan,* the big scene might not be when the Tom Hanks character is killed, but rather the fact that the Hanks character reminded him of his father, who had likewise worked doggedly as a high school English teacher for decades because he believed in the value of literature. In such a case, a donor might want to honor that legacy by making a contribution to high school education in some way, maybe through an award for great teachers.

This time, Marge says that it's the *Sound of Music,* when Julie Andrews flees to the convent.

"And what about that?" Jeff presses.

"She's banished from the children," Marge says.

"Do you have children?"

Marge shakes her head, and with an apology, she wipes away a tear.

Jeff can tell that he has hit on something very important for Marge.

To get a feeling for her other interests, Jeff asks Marge more routine questions about how she handles an everyday moral quandary like panhandlers soliciting donations on the sidewalk. "Do you usually give something, or not?"

"Almost never."

This can help determine if the donor wants to help individuals or groups. Some people care more about the bleeding man, and some care more about the bleeding community. Both are entirely legitimate; the choice is personal.

"And when you last visited someone in the hospital—how did you feel about being there?" he goes on. "Were you impressed by the medical technology, the skill of the doctors, the personal attention of the nurses? What?"

"The nurses. It seemed like they were paid so little, but they made such a difference."

"Or maybe you were struck more by the coldness of modern medicine and the expense of it all?"

"No, it was the nurses," she repeats.

All such feelings, especially the powerful ones, are strong indicators of possible areas of future commitment if she chooses to consider a contribution to health care. She might want to help fund the next generation of medical technology, or enrich the emotional environment for patients, or encourage other forms of medical care through low-tech interventions or alternative medicine.

More expansively, Jeff asks Marge how she would like to be remembered after her death.

Marge shifts in her seat and laughs uneasily.

"What would you want your eulogist to say about you? What are your enduring characteristics, the ones that left their mark? That you were kind? Generous? Shrewd?"

"Kind, I would hope. And helpful. To the next generation coming along."

That's a good guide to what she might like to create in her good works while she's alive. And it is here. It is unclear just what Marge is drawn to do with her philanthropy, but the outlines are coming into focus: it needs to have something to do with children, perhaps assisting orphans, or improving their educational options. That part will need to be more finely honed. But considering the vast world of possibilities, Marge had narrowed her interests down a lot.

Through all of this, Jeff is careful to keep his questions open-ended. Asking about a movie, he wouldn't say, "Did you react to the death because it seemed so senseless?" Rather, he'd ask, "Why did that scene move you?" While he might supply possibilities to help focus their thinking, he tries not to nudge the donors in any particular direction but lets them go wherever they are inclined, for philanthropy is about their feelings, not ours, and we need to let them surface. And because they are feelings, a donor like Marge can be reticent in talking about them. For much of the interview, Marge did not speak of them directly at all, but communicated them instead by a light that came into her eye or a fresh energy in her voice. Jeff has learned to attune himself to it. Therapists call this "listening with a third ear." In the philanthropic realm too, two ears aren't always enough.

Also, just as Jeff needs to be open in his questions, he needs to be open to their answers, whatever they might be. In philanthropy, there are no wrong answers. It is hard sometimes for donors to appreciate that fact; it is so different from everything else they are used to. In other realms, there are plenty of wrong answers—wrong because a suggestion violates company policy, wrong because we already tried that and it was a disaster, wrong because it's just plain stupid and everybody says so. Not so when it comes to philanthropic objectives. You might want to fund an antigravity machine or a museum of dust mites. There may be more constructive uses for your money, and these objectives may sound crazy, but there is nothing wrong with them. In philanthropy, the choices are not between right and wrong, but between right and right. This makes it all the harder to choose. If an option is wrong, it can be eliminated instantly. If it is right, you have to think some more, and then some more after that.

In the Cards

So far we have opened the door just a crack, allowing potential donors a narrow glimpse of what their philanthropy might be. To open that door wider, we introduce the concept of the equilateral triangle, our model of successful giving. In our triangle, each side represents one of the three essential elements: the why, the what, and the how. The why is why give? What's in it for the donor? What feelings does it elicit? The what is what's the primary area of philanthropic interest? What is the donor trying to accomplish with a gift? And the how is how to do it? What might be the mechanism, the style?

Over the years, we have developed a number of techniques to help donors think these elements through and complete this essential triangle for themselves.

Let's start with the first part of the triangle, the why. After doing this work for a few years, Jeff realized that the questions kept coming back to the underlying motivations. What did the donor really care about? What made her tick—and get ticked off? To get at that, Jeff had printed up twenty-five cards, each one bearing a motivational value, along with its definition. "Innovation—finding new and creative ways of doing things," is one. Another: "Compassion—feeling sympathy, care, or concern for others." (See the box on the next page for the full list.) Initially he planned to have the donors rank all the values, putting the cards in order from most important to least, but the donors kept getting tangled up in the middle, spending a lot of time deciding whether they'd put, say, "Leadership—Guiding people and projects; setting the pace" before or after "Responsibility—Voluntarily doing what is expected of you." He realized that it made more sense to pay attention to the extremes, to those values that the donors were most and least passionate about. So Jeff asked donors

45

to identify only their top five and bottom three and leave it at that.

Motivational Values Cards

At ACBP, we use a stack of twenty-five cards, each one displaying a value that might go into a philanthropic decision. To use them, we have a potential donor rank the cards by how significant or meaningful he finds each value. We pay particular attention to the top five and bottom three, so the donor can limit himself just to those.

These are the values:

Community: Feeling a meaningful connection to a group of people

Compassion: Feeling sympathy, care, or concern for others

Courage: Standing up in the face of fear or adversity

Effectiveness: Achieving benchmarks to accomplish goals and objectives

Equity: Being fair and free from bias

Family: Caring for and spending time with loved ones

Freedom: Having the ability to exercise choice and free will

Friendship: Experiencing close, ongoing relationships

Helping: Taking care of others and meeting their needs

Innovation: Finding new and creative ways of doing things

Integrity: Acting in alignment with your deeply held values

Justice: Pursuing what is fair and morally right

Leadership: Motivating others to work toward achieving a common purpose

---

Loyalty: Being devoted to a person, ideal, duty, or cause

Obligation: Committing to fulfill a duty or promise

Opportunity: Having the chance to progress or advance

Personal growth: Pursuing new skills and self-awareness

Pleasure: Seeking personal enjoyment

Power: Having the ability to effect change and achieve desired outcomes

Recognition: Being noted for your efforts

Responsibility: Voluntarily doing what is expected

Risk: Exploring the unknown by testing limits; being willing to fail

Spiritual growth: Seeking connection to a higher purpose

Tolerance: Respecting the beliefs, practices, or innate differences of others

Tradition: Valuing a practice, custom, or story passed down from generation to generation

To get a set of these cards, along with other resources that might be helpful for a new donor, go to the Web site of a subsidiary of ACBP, 21/64, which is devoted to issues pertaining to intergenerational philanthropy: http://www.2164.net/2164resources.html.

Interestingly enough, after hundreds of run-throughs, all the cards have made an appearance in someone's top five—all, we should say, except one: "Power—having the ability to effect change and achieve desired outcomes." No one has ever favored that, which is curious, since philanthropists do in fact wield a lot of power, and we are quite confident that many of them find it enjoyable. And among the bottom three, we've seen just about every card pop up there from time to time—but one card shows up repeatedly on the matters-least list: "Recognition—Getting noticed for your efforts." Who knew that recognition was so unimportant to so many donors? Apparently thousands of universities, hospitals, and museums had it wrong when they created so many naming opportunities.

Well, we're not sure. Attentive readers will note that Charles and his late wife, Andrea, named their foundation after themselves. And why not? This is their statement to the world about their beliefs, and there was no point in displaying any false modesty about it.

So when Jeff sees that recognition and power have been downgraded, he makes a gentle inquiry, one that usually provokes a little nervous laughter, about whether in fact the donor might actually be interested in those two qualities after all. And a helpful conversation usually follows. It's good to put all the cards on the table, for all the values and emotions they denote are potentially at play in philanthropy.

After noting the cards that aren't selected, Jeff surveys the ones that are. It can be astonishing to see the clusters of emotion that are presented as a donor's personal signature. They are quite unpredictable. Innovation, Competence, Leadership, Risk, and Responsibility might be one hard-nosed CEO's top five, and Pleasure, Personal Growth, and Tradition, his bottom three. Another equally hard-nosed CEO might put on top Tradition, Leadership, Responsibility, Integrity, and Opportunity, and put on the bottom Equality, Risk, and Community. Each pattern is legitimate, each is justifiable, and each is as unique and personal as a fingerprint.

So, what to make of it? It is important to emphasize that these are not Tarot cards, giving donors a glimpse of their future. Rather, the eight cards might be thought of as something akin to the characteristics of a new house: height, scale, location, architectural style, plot orientation, roofline, and the like. Put these together, and you might be able to generate a sketch of the house, but you could not build it. Likewise, the cards can produce only the rough outlines of a philanthropic mission; they are not a plan.

Let's take a closer look at the first cluster—the one that starts with Innovation. Often the bottom values can be at least as revealing as the top ones. And here the rejection of tradition suggests that the past is not terribly important to this donor, which is freeing. He can concentrate on the future, which is the primary focus of most philanthropy anyway. Plus, he's not into short-term satisfaction, another negative value that can have positive consequences. If there are basically three concerns in philanthropy—looking good, feeling good, and doing good—he has just eliminated one of them. He is free to charge ahead almost ruthlessly in pursuit of his ultimate goals.

What of the top values? Of the five, the first one, Innovation, may be key, so Jeff is likely to press the donor to declare what sort of innovation he is after. How would he feel if he made a million-dollar gift for a program or project that failed? That is, after all, the downside of innovation: it's risky. But risk is fine with him, giving his innovation all the more of an edge. And that, in turn, gives a certain substance to two of the other top five attributes, Competence and Responsibility, which otherwise might float off into abstraction. His philanthropy would have an edge, certainly, but not be all blade: it would also have substance and reliability. In this phase, Jeff brings in all the information available to him about the donor and might link back to the earlier point in the conversation when he said how he'd responded to a hospital visit. Not surprisingly, this rather blunt CEO hadn't been moved by seeing a patient; he'd been impressed instead by the vast array of

49

medical technology that had been brought to bear on his friend's illness. If he were to go into health care, he would probably focus on next-generation technologies that were potentially game changing. With his special interest in Competence, he would probably partner with a university or a research institute rather than relying on a start-up staffed by relatively inexperienced people.

If this is all clicking in, the donor would get animated, the ideas coming faster than before, with more hand gestures and a more forceful way of speaking. But Jeff is likely to remind him that any major change in health care is likely to occur in sawtooth fashion, with any advances quickly followed by disappointments if they occurred at all. So the donor obviously can't be guaranteed any brilliant results. Still, that risk tolerance card is likely to be taxed.

The fact is, the cards rarely yield a clear action plan. More likely, they reveal how much the donor still has to think through. But after peering into his soul in this way, at least he knows better where he's coming from, even if he can't be sure yet where he is going.

Now, What to Do?

But let's say our donor is ready to move on and start zeroing in on a program area for his philanthropy. For this, there are no cards to assist him. We once figured out that there are about 150 general areas for giving: environmental preservation, reproductive rights, and art appreciation are just a few examples, and those are merely the subject headings. When you get down into subspecialties where the actual work is done, there are tens of thousands more. (More about this later.) It's a little like picking a wine. It's one thing to decide if you want a Bordeaux or a Chardonnay, but it's quite another to select the vineyard and the vintage.

Still, it is possible to make some headway. Say you have a big interest in the arts. Well, why? What drives that? For one person, perhaps it was that his father was a major donor to the Metropolitan Museum of Art, and he was always close to his father and inspired by him. Another person might be drawn to the wild parties that the art scene is known for, and she finds it a total thrill to mingle with the city's rich and artistic element. A third might be an amateur painter who has found that his art has rounded out his life in a meaningful way. Each of these connections would dictate a different sort of involvement: the first toward expanding museum collections, the second toward a gift that would secure membership on a board, the third on funding some kind of enrichment program for an underserved audience. If you use the series of questions revealed in the first interview and in the cluster of values cards, you may be a little quicker to see what sort of work you're drawn to.

Another way for a donor to jump-start her thinking is to think about who her philanthropic heroes are and why. If it's Bill Gates, is it because of his practical-mindedness, the reach of his activities, or the humanitarian focus? Or if it's John D. Rockefeller, is it because of his interest in universities or his preservationism? For Andrew Carnegie, is it his focus on libraries or maybe his belief in learning? All of these questions can trigger some compelling associations.

Or he could go to a large federated charity like the United Way or the Jewish Federation and check out the programs they offer. Each is a kind of department store with a wide variety of philanthropic offerings. It can be useful to see them in action, get a sense of the operation, the recipients, the delivery system, and see—and feel—what appeals. A science-oriented after-school program perhaps? Meals-on-wheels for shut-ins? Language classes for immigrants?

Another way is to flip through some magazines to see which photographs catch your eye. Magazine photographs reveal much of the world, and so many varieties of the people in it, that they serve as a kind of catalogue of philanthropic possibilities. Are you captivated by images of a drought-lowered lake or an earthquake-ravaged city? Moved by a desolate farm or a decaying urban neighborhood? An archaeological dig or some scientific expedition? A bikini-clad celebrity or a victim of famine? All of these subjects suggest a potential subject for philanthropy, even the celebrity: she could arouse interest in body image issues for teenaged girls, or media distortions of desire, or infinite other possibilities.

In watching people flip through the magazine photographs, Jeff has often been struck by how often people are drawn to what they are not. Time and again, a heavy-set woman will single out a photograph of a slim model, and a confirmed city dweller will linger over pictures of the wilderness. Philanthropy, after all, is by nature aspirational. The philanthropist considers the world not so much as it is but as she wishes it would be. Wants, hankerings, longings—all are instructive and not to be discounted, because they can signal that deep place within from which the most committed philanthropy can spring. This is a more complicated aspiration in play too. Often those two desires—on the global level and the personal level—are linked, for in trying to transform the world, the philanthropist is trying to change herself too: She is turning herself into a person who would do such a good deed. These triggers deepen the self-conversation about both strategy and image further. (For more information about the psychological tools developed at ACBP, see http://www.2164.net/2164resources.html.)

It's Not How You Feel; It's How You Look

Through these first two stages, a donor's investigations are likely to produce a few eureka moments. The exercises also help hone the concept, so that the donor can close in on that elusive area of profound interest. With that in mind, we turn to the third side of the triangle: the means and style of the donor's giving.

There are many ways of delivering philanthropy, depending on how much of an infrastructure the donor wants, and we will treat them in greater detail later on. For now, we'll touch on just the basics. The simplest form of philanthropy, of course, is to write a check to your favorite nonprofit. The next simplest is the donor-advised fund, which grew significantly in popularity about ten to fifteen years ago. Started in Cleveland, community foundations offered donors a continued involvement in their philanthropy. Essentially a philanthropic investment account, these funds are now also available at Fidelity, Schwab, and a number of other large investment houses. The donor makes a tax-deductible gift and then recommends distributions from that gift to the nonprofits of his choice. Then there is the private foundation that has no staff, just the donor and the endowment he has contributed. Such a foundation is attractive to individuals who have sold a business, for instance, and want to avoid paying the capital gains but want to retain control of these philanthropic assets. The proceeds can be placed in a private foundation tax free, the only Internal Revenue Service stipulation being that at least 5 percent of its assets are spent on charitable purposes each year. These unstaffed foundations are extremely common now, representing the overwhelming majority of the seventy-six thousand foundations in existence. Finally, there is the staffed family foundation, like Charles's, which maintains at least a small staff. (His has twenty-one.) Although a minority of foundations fall into this category, it is the type of philanthropy that most people think of because it includes such heavyweights as the Ford and Rockefeller foundations.

Those are the basic forms that philanthropy can take. But what about the style? While characteristics like traditional or hip may seem superficial, they in fact go to the heart of the operation, just as an individual's flair reveals more about him than his build. To get at it, Jeff often asks donors which historical figure they most admire. Oddly enough, both genders tend to select males, and the most common choices are Winston Churchill, Albert Schweitzer, and John F. Kennedy. But, of course, it is more interesting to find out why these are the choices, and the standard associations are not always the ones that donors connect with. It may not necessarily be Kennedy's fabled charisma, for instance, that catches a donor, but his relative youth, his confident liberalism, or, for some, his graceful acceptance of his back pain that strikes the chord. Such elements are helpful. If it is the youth that is so appealing, it suggests any foundation should have a "new kid on the block" attitude; the liberalism encourages a political stance such as the one espoused by the Brookings Institution; and the pain may encourage attending to the hurting parts of society. It can help to think about cars too. Cars are useful vehicles—so to speak—for a flight of fancy because each is the product of such an elaborate and pervasive marketing campaign that everyone can agree, pretty much, on what each style represents, and in their variety, they cover the full psychosocial spectrum.

There is obviously a world of cars to pick from, but for convenience, Jeff limits the choices to nine: Jeep, Ferrari, Mercedes, Oldsmobile, pickup truck, Range Rover, Rolls Royce, tank, and Volkswagen. Some of these, like the tank, are playful, but they are there to demonstrate the wide range of possibilities for foundations. One size does not fit all.

The clear favorites are the Mercedes and the Jeep, possibly because they represent the two extremes. No one has yet picked a Rolls Royce, but then few drivers do either. Mercedes, of course, is all about the status that is bound up in the car's reputation for quality, comfort, reliability—and expense. A Mercedes-type foundation would be one that would be expected to be stable, smoothly running, and classy. And it would be expected to spend whatever it costs to achieve its objectives in terms of staff and program. Some donors forget about that last part, and Jeff has to remind them that quality doesn't come cheap. If they want Mercedes, they'll have to pay for it.

When people decide they're drawn to a Jeep, Jeff sometimes wonders if they really want to create a private foundation at all. Jeeps, after all, are not just rough and ready, but they are also stripped down, frill free, and, compared to a full-fledged SUV, are relatively inexpensive. So he sometimes asks them why they don't turn to a donor-advised fund instead, for such a fund is really the Jeep of philanthropies—ultraefficient, just a chassis with a gas pedal.

Charles's wife Andrea realized she was basically a Jeep, but she wanted a steering wheel—one she alone could wield: limited boards of directors, little staff, focused purpose. (Tellingly, when she was asked her role model, she picked Moses, who didn't have a board of directors or much of a staff either.) So back in 2001, when she trying to think what she could do for the families of the victims of 9/11, she decided she wanted to give them the balm of the city's culture—its art, music, ballet, and theater. Thus was born The Gift of New York, a program that would provide free tickets to cultural, sports, and entertainment events and venues to family members of those lost, as part of the healing process. It had a board of five, each with an area of expertise and impressive list of contacts. As planned, after eighteen months, the program, and the organization with it, ended. The Gift of New York served ten thousand grateful family members whose children were able to smile, often for the first time after September 11, at the circus or a Yankees game. Spare as Andrea's organization was, its purpose was magnificent, and she certainly did make a difference in the lives of families affected by the tragedy.

Ready?

To paraphrase Churchill, this is not the beginning of the end, but the end of the beginning. Thus far we have established the donor's disposition and orientation. He is probably not ready to go out and rent office space, but he does know which way is forward and how to proceed. For too many novice philanthropists, the sequence is not ready, aim, fire! It's fire, aim, ready. Or, for some, it's ready, aim, aim, aim, aim. As with so many activities that require vision, it can take a little while to focus. Would-be philanthropists peer out at this vast world of need and see mostly a blur of smudgy colors. But in time, and with some effort, certain parts of this world will start to clarify and exert a certain unmistakable pull. Our techniques can hasten this process, but they are not guaranteed to yield The Thing—that subject of consuming passion—promptly, and they almost certainly won't deliver it in the few minutes that it has taken you to read this chapter. No, these are lengthy practices, as the Buddhists say, but if you keep your mind open, that moment of clarity will come. And when it does, you'll be amazed. You'll wonder how you could have ever failed to see it. The answer is, you were looking in the wrong place. It was never out there, not really; it was inside you the whole time, buried down deep where the truest things lie.

CHAPTER 6

Accelerants

SMALL CHANGES CAN MAKE POWERFUL DIFFERENCES in the world—if you know what to change and how to change it. It's all a matter of leverage, of finding a way to intercede with a manageable force so that it achieves the maximum good. Much of philanthropy is concerned with direct service—the actual delivery of the goods. The hospital, the museum, the theater company, the community center: these are the public side of philanthropy, where needs are served. But to another way of thinking, they are a little late in the game.

We like the parable of the two men who see a series of people drowning in a river. One responds by jumping in to save each person. The other races upstream to try to keep any more people from falling in. This is the essential dilemma in philanthropy: whether to address consequences or causes. Dealing with the consequences takes care of immediate needs. Locating the root causes can be much harder but can yield far more profound and sweeping results.

How can the donor get down to that level, where his contribution achieves maximum results?

Let's count the ways.

Advocates

Consider the initiatives of the past half-century that have emerged from the civil rights movement and reflect the best of our attempts to create a more perfect society. Countless organizations have advocated for the rights of other minorities, of women, of gay people. One of the most sweeping pieces of legislation in the postwar era, the Americans with Disabilities Act, shifted social attitudes regarding the disabled as it mandated special ramps, parking spaces, seating, reasonable accommodations at the workplace, and much else for them. Or think of NARAL, the pro-choice organization that advocates in thirty states. It is a force in presidential elections and is a major reason that abortion is still legal in the United States. One political bill. One organization. Each has yielded returns in national policy that far exceed the incremental costs to even the most generous donor. And behind each of them lies a dedicated team of advocates, funded at least in part by donors who saw a point of leverage where they could create a large change in society for a relatively small amount of money.

The Targeted Gift for Marketing

But there are plenty of other high-leverage interventions that venture upstream to make the changes that yield the greatest long-term impact. A targeted gift for assistance in marketing is one that can dramatically increase the reach and effectiveness of a nonprofit. All too often, when times are tough (as they virtually always are), nonprofits cut back on such expenditures because they don't dare touch anything else. A philanthropist can take up the slack and kick in, say, for a specific marketing campaign, which then could well pay for itself in new clients, patrons, or customers.

Take the local dance troupe that is playing to half-full houses. If a donor funds a $100,000 marketing campaign that succeeds in filling those seats, generating maybe $500,000 in revenue, she will have leveraged her gift at five to one.

One caveat: the donor should make clear that hers is a one-time gift. The dance troupe can't take her for a lady bountiful who'll cover all budgetary shortfalls indefinitely. She should insist that the first $100,000 in tickets fund next year's marketing budget.

Or take the needs of a small, deserving nonprofit like a start-up inner-city basketball league. It might have a budget of $100,000 a year, but when seeking foundation support that would lift it to the next level, it is stymied because it can't afford the independent audit that foundations generally require of any potential recipient. A strategic philanthropist, however, can donate the $10,000 for the audit, which then qualifies the league for more substantial support.

Supporting Infrastructure

Useful as it is to work from without, by applying incentives and direction to nonprofits, you can also work from within by enhancing the existing capabilities of the organization at hand. Technical assistance, for example, allows staffers to get more out of their Excel spreadsheets, database management systems, and search functions. Infrastructural support can be as simple as improving a building's insulation to cut heating bills, but such a gift can make all the difference to an organization on the financial edge. Legal assistance can be critical to the survival of an organization that has been hit by a lawsuit or is fighting to get full benefits for some elderly clients that had illegally been denied them. In a case of a sweeping denial of rights, a class action suit can improve the lives of thousands.

For some organizations, organizations are already in place that are designed to offer them assistance, and they may be worth financial support. If you are concerned about the effectiveness of your local United Way, for instance, you can give it some help by supporting a national organization, United Way of America, which offers support and instruction to individual United Ways to boost their performance. Or instead of giving to just your local hospital, you could support your local hospital association, which supplies an array of services to a cluster of hospitals, expanding the impact of your gift.

A Prize

A Nobel Prize marks the glorious culmination of a career and is a goal for virtually every working scientist. But many other lesser-known prizes have their own allure, shifting people's interests and behavior into alignment with the prize's creator. Why not create, or contribute toward, a prize that advances your own social, scientific, or literary agenda? As it is, there is the X Prize, sponsored by various corporate interests to encourage such efforts as placing a robot on the moon or developing a hyperefficient automobile. With prize money placed at $10 million and up, the incentives are substantial and the potential value to humanity tremendous. The Templeton Prize recognizes the thinker who best unifies science and religion. Charles's two adult children have created the $100,000 Charles Bronfman Prize to recognize extraordinary humanitarians under age fifty, with the hope that they will become role models for others and that the attention will widen the impact of their work. Prize winners, in addition to getting a cash award, received a burst of publicity that drew attention to their work and their accomplishments. Tissue matching for transplants, protecting women refugees fleeing Darfur—such initiatives and others have been recognized by the prize.

Some prizes are intended to stimulate entrepreneurs to produce work of special value to the prize giver; others are meant to honor those who have already done so. But either way, they set a standard for performance in a realm of some significance and can have a profoundly transformative effect.

All of these approaches—from advocacy and marketing through to legal assistance and prize giving—fall under the general category of accelerants. Like fuel on a fire, they boost the energy in the nonprofit system, speeding up the pace of change, increasing the number of clients served, and benefiting from the attention and cross-fertilization that results.

Gifts for Creating and Meeting Standards

While many of the other accelerants operate from below, offering an extra boost to an organization in need, other incentives take a different approach and provide lofty goals for them to aspire to. One would be through the creation of national standards for nonprofit boards, a critical measurement that does not yet exist. That may seem slight and technical, but it would have enormous repercussions in the nonprofit world, especially for smaller operations that are less well versed in best practices. National standards would establish the optimum number of board meetings per year, say, or minimum requirements for board attendance, or term limits, or annual contributions, and proper configuration of subcommittees, and the like.

But outside of board operations, virtually every realm of philanthropy could benefit from the establishment of useful state-of-the-art standards and from helping every organization meet them. In health care, for instance, there's already a Joint Commission on the Accreditation of Health Care Organizations, but too often the individual health clinic can't afford the accreditation process. What's more, in the scramble to keep up with daily business, the clinic may not have kept adequate records or has fallen short of standards in small ways, like failing to have a thermometer in every refrigerator as required. A donor might step in with support for moving the clinic to accreditation so that any extra funds it acquires can go to meeting the standards of the accreditation. Thus, that initial donation serves as a powerful accelerator, vaulting that clinic up to the next level in efficiency, credibility, and reliability.

A major issue in the health care industry is the cyclical shortage of nurses. One of the reasons cited for the current shortage is that since 9/11, fewer immigrants have been admitted into the country from the Philippines, Ireland, and other countries that had always provided a significant percentage of the nurses in the United States. A number of strategies can increase the number of nurses. Advocate for increased immigration for potential nurses. Press for funding for tuition, books, and lab fees so that nurses' aides and other promising hospital staff can be retrained as nurses. Increase the number of nursing faculty and the resources available to nursing education. Or start a nursing school, like the Helene Fuld School of Nursing in New Jersey, which was founded in the 1880s by a wealthy woman who was determined to create more nurses. The first step for the strategic donor is to better understand why there is a nursing shortage. Funds spent on research often save the expense of going down the wrong road. Foundations concerned with health care like the Robert Wood Johnson Foundation and benefactors like the Sandler and Jonas families have recently come to the same conclusion and pursued all of these approaches.

It also requires a degree of responsiveness on the part of the nonprofit to recognize the value of what its donors are offering. And that value is not always measured in dollars. Years ago, when the firebrand Louis Farrakhan was at the height of his influence, an antibigotry nonprofit ran an ad opposing him in the *New York Times.* That was considered daring, but the ad was well executed and highly effective. A New Yorker we'll call Herb was impressed with the ad and followed up with a ten thousand dollar donation. In many organizations, such an unsolicited check would get lost in the bureaucracy, but at this one, it was quickly brought to the attention of the executive director. When he called Herb to thank him, he said that the organization didn't get unsolicited checks of that size every day. Would he be willing to have lunch? Herb said he'd be delighted. At lunch, Herb discovered that the executive director was seriously overweight. Concerned about the director's health and vitality both for the man's own sake and for the sake of the organization he headed, Herb offered to take him to a Pritikin residential health and longevity center to improve his health. Just to protect his investment, Herb told him. But in fact Herb had located an essential point of leverage, since this executive was indeed essential to the welfare of the organization, and it ran much more efficiently and smartly when the executive director was at optimal health. His gift of a stay at Pritikin was probably as valuable as the six-figure gift Herb was also bestowing.

In philanthropy, there is a supply side, and there is a demand side. On the supply side stands a donor ready to give, and on the demand side is a development office eager to receive. Usually the two meet somewhere in the middle. But this particular transaction all started with Herb, and that is the attitude we would like to encourage, for it embodies the best of the New Philanthropy. It is okay to respond to entreaties from nonprofits; to a large degree, that is essential. But it is better to think them up on your own and decide for yourself what, deep down, you really want to do. Again, the more of yourself you put in, the more you will get out. Either way, you are giving your money. But only when you stay on the supply side are you fully giving yourself: your inspiration, your dedication, your passion. This, again, is the joy of giving.

CHAPTER 7

Finding Your Niche

THE UNIVERSE OF PHILANTHROPY IS AS VAST as the heavens. There are so many potential gifts of so many varieties for so many causes. In Chapter Six, we tried to help the potential donor locate her own unique philanthropic desire within the vast welter of possible motivations. With this chapter, we'll try to knock this other universe of possibility down to size.

Again, the possibilities here are enormous. It would take a book the size of the New York telephone directory to describe just a sliver of one realm of giving. In an effort to broadly categorize all nonprofit organizations, the National Center for Charitable Statistics created the National Taxonomy of Exempt Entities classification system, doing for philanthropy what Linnaeus did for the animal kingdom: it is the industry-wide standard for nonprofit organizational classification. (www.artofgivingbook.com contains the complete taxonomy.)

For philanthropy, the matter is no less complex, and it gets all the more so as you descend to ever-finer levels of distinction between one type of cause and another. But just the broad outlines are daunting, as we see here in the broad overview in Table 7.1 of the twenty-six essential categories, from the Arts to the intriguingly titled Unknown.

Table 7.1. Overview of the National Taxonomy of Exempt Entities: Core Codes Classification System, 2005

A	Arts, Culture & Humanities
B	Education
C	Environment
D	Animal-Related
E	Health Care
F	Mental Health & Crisis Intervention
G	Diseases, Disorders & Medical Disciplines
H	Medical Research
I	Crime & Legal-Related
J	Employment
K	Food, Agriculture & Nutrition
L	Housing & Shelter
M	Public Safety, Disaster Preparedness & Relief
N	Recreation & Sports
O	Youth Development
P	Human Services
Q	International, Foreign Affairs & National Security
R	Civil Rights, Social Action & Advocacy
S	Community Improvement & Capacity Building
T	Philanthropy, Voluntarism & Grantmaking Foundations
U	Science & Technology
V	Social Science
W	Public & Societal Benefit
X	Religion-Related
Y	Mutual & Membership Benefit
Z	Unknown

SOURCE: Used with permission, National Center for Charitable Statistics.

At the other extreme, take a category like health, and zoom in to the actual subject areas where the work takes place, and you find, just for the diseases of the eye, for example:

- Disorders of the eyelid, lacrimal system, and orbit
- Disorders of the conjunctiva
- Disorders of the sclera, cornea, iris, and ciliary body
- Disorders of lens
- Disorders of choroid and retina
- Glaucoma
- Disorders of vitreous body and globe
- Disorders of optic nerve and visual pathways
- Disorders of ocular muscles, binocular movement, accommodation, and refraction
- Visual disturbances and blindness

We could go on for many, many pages. In the medical field, virtually every illness has attracted a cluster of nonprofits to support its victims, fund its causes, and develop treatments. And this is just one portion of one portion of one portion of one portion of philanthropy.

The Dimensions of Philanthropy

One way to begin to get a handle on all the possibilities is to imagine it spatially. Think of all of philanthropy as one huge cube whose dimensions are not height, length, and width but population, field, and mode of service.

What could all this possibly mean?

Population

Let's start with population: the group of people to be served. It could be any group, from elderly Eskimos to the urban poor. But it is important to recognize that the group that is served is human, even if the cause itself is not. It is, after all, philanthropy, the love of humankind as we've said, not the love of plant life or astrology. The cause may be the Brazilian rain forest, stray cats, the quilts of western Missouri, or the history of ideas, but the population in question is the people who will benefit from advances in these causes, whether it is by the discovery of new medicines in the rain forest, the improved sense of decency for those protecting stray cats, the uplift from seeing the beautiful quilts, or the thrill of tracing the history of ideas. With all of them, humanity is the measure.

Field

The work inevitably must be broken down further if it is to be meaningful, and a key element is its field, or topic. While a population is usually quite vast, involving thousands, if not millions, of individuals, a field can be almost infinitely particularized depending on how finely you want to slice it. It is rather like the way matter can be broken down to molecules and ultimately to subatomic particles and many levels below that. A large category like "education" can be cut down to early childhood education or vocational training or many other kinds of education, and then can be further refined from there. "Health" could be Alzheimer's disease research, fitness programs, cholesterol reduction, and a million others, to say nothing of their many sub-sub-categories. "Poverty," likewise, can be interpreted as rural poverty of the American South, cultural deprivation, malnutrition, and many, many more. And of course they have their subsets too.

Mode of Service

Once the other major questions are resolved and you know the individuals affected and the area of activity, you need to decide how you are to get involved. That's the issue of mode of service. Would you want to be involved directly or indirectly in the delivery of, say, treatment of gastrointestinal disease? Direct treatment would occur at a hospital or clinic, with an individual patient. Indirect treatment would take place elsewhere, involving research on these diseases, finding out how GI diseases are handled from a policy perspective, or focusing on interventions or palliatives. Or you might want to shift away from managing the disease and get involved with some research effort, policy advocacy, or marketing effort.

Compared to population and field, mode of service is the area of philanthropy that may require the greatest contemplation. You will need to ponder the whole long production line of an issue, from its many original sources through to its final outcome, to decide where and how to intervene. Mothers Against Drunk Drivers surveyed the issue of dangerous drinking and decided that the best point of engagement was back up the chain of causal connections. They would change the culture of drinking by creating a whole new member of the party, the designated driver—a term this group popularized—who will chauffeur the drinkers safely home.

When Charles wanted to do something for the Israel Philharmonic, he split his gift in two. With one portion he enabled the orchestra to purchase a number of world-class violins. That was for the Philharmonic of today. With the other, he arranged for what were termed Concerts in Jeans, which would start after the regular concert ended and be free to young people. That was for the Philharmonic of tomorrow.

Using the Dimensions

With each of these three dimensions representing one sliver of possibility, their intersection—two of them crossing to produce a line, and then the third slicing through to produce a dot along that line—can allow you to pinpoint exactly what it is that you want to do. If you decide, for instance, that you care most about small children, that's one slice: the population. But then you might think about what need or issue you would like to address. And you remember your deep passion for the arts—one that was fostered by the pleasure your mother took painting watercolors, and you identify that as your field: artistic appreciation in the very young. And finally, for mode of delivery, you think about elementary schools and decide that the best way to promote art appreciation is to work up a curriculum for art teachers with young students. When you have identified that third slice—supporting art teachers—you have located the exact spot in the philanthropic universe where you want to be. It is the point where the three planes of your interest intersect. Its specificity, its uniqueness matches yours. It is a chance for you to brand yourself and become known for something—and, if you do it right, that something will express a lot of who you are.

To Give Is to Choose

In the example, the donor began with her interest in small children. But you can enter this cube on any face—starting with population, field, or mode of service. It really doesn't matter which. Few people start by considering all the possibilities—the thousands of disease entities in health care and nearly as many choices in education, just to take two—and winnowing them down. Instead, most people realize they have an urge to do some particular thing—a notion that might be encouraged by our values cards—and they plunge in. That self-knowledge narrows the choices significantly and makes them much easier to make. Again, philanthropy starts with you.

If your mother recently died of breast cancer, that might well be a point of orientation for you. You are determined to keep other women from sharing that same fate. That would immediately suggest a certain narrowly defined population: women who are at risk for breast cancer. Shifting the lens a bit, you may take as your population the children who are left behind after the cancer, mourning their mother's loss. Or you might come at it in another of the three dimensions of our cube and concentrate on the field of breast cancer itself. That could lead to a particular mode of service, like research into techniques of pain management, for example, if that aspect of your mother's care had been seriously deficient, or postoperative care. There are still many choices to make, but many fewer than you faced initially.

Here's a Trick

You have to start somewhere, and once you do get started, you have a better chance of deciding what it really is you want to do. It's almost as if that initial burst of enthusiasm for a particular approach sets you on a trajectory that will take you to your target. There will be some refinement along the way.

We came up with an interesting exercise in 1997 when we were trying to decide among a variety of potential initiatives in the early stage of the Andrea and Charles Bronfman Philanthropies. We were focusing primarily on the notions of enhancing Canadianism and of Jewish peoplehood. These were fields that suggested populations, but they were not modes of service. Although they addressed the questions of *for whom* and *what,* they didn't address the key matter of *how* the work was to be done.

To analyze different possibilities on the Jewish peoplehood side, we dummied up an issue of a wire service daily report of the Jewish Telegraphic Agency that was dated three years into the future. It consisted of eighteen one-paragraph stories, all of them news events that might have stemmed from one interpretation of the initiative or another. One was a report from a conference of "Future World Jewish Leaders" in Geneva, another some spot news on the awarding of a "Bronfman Prize for Jewish Unity" in the Jerusalem Theater, and a third the announcement of a competition for a $100,000 award of early development money for filmmakers interested in advancing Jewish connections. Brief as each story was, it was detailed and evocative enough that the reader might see the implications of the different angles on this initiative.

The trustees were then asked to rank these stories on three dimensions: importance, potential impact, and personal resonance. In the end, the stories were enormously helpful, and one story jumped out above all the others: the report headlined "20,000 Teens in Israel," and it scored highly on every dimension of the cube we have been describing. It had just the right population, field, and mode of service. And from it came the strong commitment to creating the Birthright Israel program that was launched two years later.

One Donor's Route

Formerly the CEO of Overseas Shipholding Group, one of the largest fleets of oil tankers, Morton P. Hyman went on to head up MPH Enterprises, an investment firm where he exercised his talents as a value investor. Something of a value investor on the social side as well, he had always been a community leader, having served as chairman of Beth Israel Medical Center and founding chairman of Continuum, the holding company that resulted from the combination of Beth Israel, St. Luke's-Roosevelt, New York Eye and Ear Infirmary, and other medical resources in New York. When his terms were up, he was thinking about the next philanthropic challenge when he happened to read a caption accompanying a photo of a blind woman in Africa in the *New York Times*. It said that trachoma, better known as river blindness, could be eliminated for fifty cents a person. *Fifty cents,* he thought. *That would make a very solid value investment.* So he started with trachoma and connected to the Sabin Institute, which he now chairs: its global network treated over 150 million people last year. The institute, which also develops new vaccines, is now also supported by major grants from the Gates Foundation.

Tempting as it is in philanthropy as in other areas of life, you can't just "go for it," as the expression is. At every stage, you need to stop and think if this is the right project for you and one that can really work. In the case of the man whose mother has died of breast cancer, he needs to be realistic. If he has only $100,000 at his disposal, he can't very well hope to cure breast cancer. But he could make a more modest contribution that would nonetheless be extremely meaningful, for example, sponsoring self-help groups for the breast cancer patients or their families, who are struggling with the disease. Every philanthropic gift is subject to constraints—financial ones, primarily. But there are also matters of feasibility, timing, politics, and technology, for example. Dozens of issues may well have a heavy bearing on the nature and usefulness of the gift, and the donor had best consider them before making his gift, not after. Consult with people in the field, read up, and review the market. Do your due diligence. You'll regret it if you don't.

Slicing the Pie

You've just seen how we might approach this matter of choosing our cause. How do most Americans do it? What causes are they most drawn to? The statistics reach down only to the broadest categories. But for a general idea, take a look at the data from the Giving USA Foundation, which, in conjunction with the Center on Philanthropy at Indiana University, publishes an annual report on giving in the United States, shown in Figure 7.1.

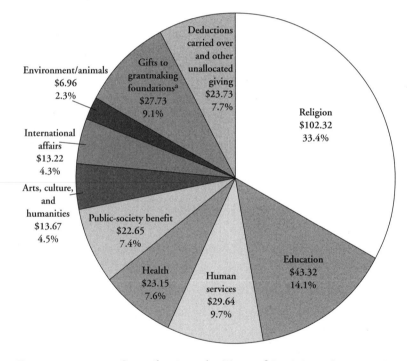

Figure 7.1. 2007 Contributions, by Type of Recipient Organization

Note: In billions of dollars. The year total is $306.39 billion. All figures are rounded. Total may not be 100 percent.

[a]Foundation Center and *Giving USA* estimate.

SOURCE: *Giving USA 2008*, Giving USA Foundation™.

By far the thickest slice of the pie, almost 34 percent, goes to religion. Education is a distant second at 14 percent of total giving, followed by human services at just under 10 percent. Strikingly, Americans give to causes that support themselves and people like them. Religious gifts, for example, are overwhelmingly to the religion of the donor and college donations to the colleges of the donor. The gifts to the poor are a prominent exception, where the better human instincts recognizing need outweigh the mirror effect in philanthropy.

Foundations, which account for 13 percent of total giving, have a far different impression of the needs of society, as Figure 7.2 shows. For this, religion drops to the smallest slice of the pie at a scant 2.3 percent, and health vaults to the top of the list at 24.5 percent, followed closely by education at 22.5, then public society benefit at 14.1 percent, human services at 13.0 percent, the arts at 11.6 percent, and so on, as you see.

As a demonstration, perhaps, of their determination to address need wherever it is located, American foundations have boosted their giving mostly to causes overseas. Donors have come to recognize that it is important to influence change in Asia, Africa, and the Middle East. And there are plenty of foundations that have specialized in giving domestically where it is needed most.

To us, Julius Rosenwald is one of the greatest philanthropists in the United States, and also one of the most unheralded. Best known for creating modern-day Sears Roebuck, he also took an enormous interest in the plight of African Americans across the South and established a foundation to create a series of colleges intended exclusively for the education of black students—over 600,000 in all—at a time when they had few alternatives. The foundation also backed a half-dozen prominent black universities such as Tuskegee, Howard, and Fisk.

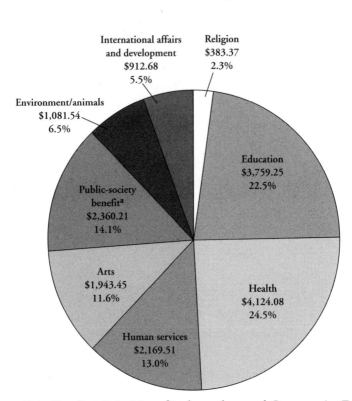

Figure 7.2. Funding Priorities of Independent and Community Foundations, 2006 ($ millions)

[a]Includes amounts for science and technology and for social science, reported separately by the Foundation Center in *Foundation Giving Trends* (2008), based on a sample of foundations.

SOURCE: *Giving USA 2008*, Giving USA Foundation™.

The Rose Foundation does something similar in New York, seeking out exceptionally talented sixth graders who are growing up in challenging social environments. The Rose Foundation's ambition is to get these kids into Ivy League schools. In addition to providing education tools, it also helps these children over the other hurdles, whether it's finding them a sports jacket to wear to college interviews or paying for math tutors. When the children are selected by the foundation, the parents are invited for a small ceremony in which each family is presented with a bonsai tree. The message is, "As beautiful as the tree is, it was stunted by its environment. See that your tree grows to its full height."

Finding The Thing

The decision about where to invest your philanthropic money is not likely to be made in one swoop. A tentative notion might lead to vigorous enthusiasm followed by anxious reconsideration and scornful rejection. From its ashes, another idea might spring up to suffer the same fate or emerge as The Thing. It's a process of exploration and retrenchment and then exploration again. All the stars in the galaxy of nonprofit ideas are never under full consideration. But the donor shouldn't limit herself to just one or two either. It is a big world out there, and donors might be astonished to discover the satisfaction of connecting to some distant corner of it. A wealthy, sophisticated entrepreneur supporting the cause of educating southern blacks: the link might be mysterious, but the payoff for both sides is not. With the Rosenwald example in mind, we encourage donors to stretch. It's the only way they can grow.

PART TWO

The Partners

"Never choose a mission statement on a dark, rainy day."

CHAPTER 8

Do I Do It — or Do I Buy It?

ONCE YOU HAVE SETTLED ON A PARTICULAR undertaking, you have to decide how best to achieve it. Do you go out into the world and start doing it yourself—or do you buy into some existing organization that is already doing something similar?

It doesn't take too much thought to identify the main characteristics of the two sides of this dilemma. Doing it yourself is where the glory is. Everyone loves a hero who goes it alone, against all odds, and all the more so if he is bent on creating something to the benefit of everyone. You're Thomas Edison or a Wright brother, an inventor, a person who brings to the world something new and needed, a brand that represents originality.

The idea, though, is just the start. You need to deliver the product, and that isn't always easy, especially for a maverick. There's finding office space, building a staff, managing budgets, determining procedures, establishing performance measures and monitoring them, and on and on. It could easily take hundreds and hundreds of hours before you helped your first person, if you ever do. By contrast, if you tap into an existing organization, all you have to do is write the check and you're in business.

Do you want to be an entrepreneur or an investor? Do you do, or do you buy? The two fall into two personality types, ones that will seem familiar from the for-profit world. In the nonprofit world, the classic entrepreneur type is Bill Gates, who has spent billions creating his foundation and then ramping it up to global scale. The classic investor type is Warren Buffett. He liked what Gates was doing and wrote his foundation a rather large check. Typically, the entrepreneur is passionate, if not fiery. The investor is likely to be quieter and more methodical. The entrepreneur is often younger, full of energy, tolerant of risks. The investor is generally older, happy to go more slowly, and inclined toward security.

Of course, the divide is not always so stark. Philanthropic investors have gradations of involvement. They can invest their money, or they can invest themselves. And in investing themselves, they can do that at a wide range of levels, from a volunteer tour guide to board chair, just as an employee of a for-profit firm can operate at anywhere from the entry level up to senior management. But it's a lot harder on the nonprofit side. The nonprofit volunteer needs infinitely greater people skills, a better sense of touch, and an intuitive sense for organizational procedures that may not be evident from any flowchart.

One Observation About Nonprofit Boards

Years ago, when Jeff was working at the New York Federation, the budget director was a man named Friedman. And the senior staff developed what it termed FLOG: Friedman's Law On Grants. The law stated that there was an inverse relationship between the size of the grant and the amount of time spent discussing it. The grants process was labor intensive, with many meetings and site visits. However, if they were to consider a massive $6 million grant to a family service agency, it would often be approved with the most cursory discussion. But when it came to deciding about the $17,000 for a new van to a community center, everyone had an opinion, and it could take hours. Why? A figure in the millions is somehow abstract, so there is little to say about it. A figure in the thousands is quite concrete, so everyone has an opinion. This isn't sensible or even prudent, but it is human nature.

A Caution

If you've been a for-profit entrepreneur, you may think you're well prepared to be a social one. Think again. There are many reasons that this might not be so, starting with your temperament and the culture of the nonprofit world. But consider the practical ones, too, like where the money comes from. The for-profit entrepreneur can qualify for loans from a bank to fund basic operations and then, once a record of financial performance is established, he might seek more money to scale up. Not so for the social entrepreneur, who has to provide his own money or turn to friends and relatives, and then bring out the tin cup for any further funding. The for-profit entrepreneur may well get his funds from the first bank he tries, if he is going to get them at all. No bank will give a loan to anyone dreaming of starting up a nonprofit, for there are no projected revenues, only liabilities. And that can get frustrating if, say, you are desperate to help the people dying of AIDS in sub-Saharan Africa and a bank won't kick in a penny.

And then, if you do succeed, you have to play yet a different role. On the for-profit side, the successful entrepreneur becomes an owner, and we all know what that is. On the nonprofit side, the entrepreneur becomes a steward, a hallowed but mysterious role that is much harder to get. It involves keeping in mind the larger purpose of the enterprise while satisfying its many stakeholders—all the "customers" who are being served, the clients, the donors, the board, the regulators and other funders, the staff. And he has to reward these backers in ways that go well beyond the return on investment that is produced on the for-profit side. He does this by letting them know what a difference they are making in the world and by letting them in on the decision making. That is not nearly as easy as handing them a monetary return.

Partnering

At the Bronfman Philanthropies, we have certainly partnered on many other projects, since our partners have enabled us to expand our reach much further than we could ever go ourselves. For us, partnership means leverage, and it is the key reason we have been able to produce over $200 million worth of programs a year with an investment of under $20 million. With Birthright Israel, we and a partner started it for $16 million; eight years later, we still give over $2 million a year, but now it has an annual budget of over $100 million, an investment that obviously dwarfs our own.

But much as we appreciate our partners, we have given up something to join with them. Each partner you take on requires some compromise since their objectives are rarely in perfect alignment with yours. No two people ever see things the same way, and that is all the more true of two organizations. To buy into the program was to buy into an organization's guiding principles. Without them, partners would have insisted that we give up the "gift" nature of the program, tie into operational partnerships that were less efficient and entrepreneurial, and spend less on research and evaluation. The compromises to date have been relatively benign, such as the typeface of the logo and the nature of partnership recognition. Too many partners can inhibit bold programming, as consensus is often the enemy of innovation. Even beyond the inevitable incongruity in objectives, it is also rare to find a match in cultures, effectiveness, talent, and approach. So then the question becomes: Do the benefits of partnership outweigh the costs? Can you accomplish your objectives better in combination, or by going forth on your own?

Going It Alone

There are times when you have to start your own. To get Birthright going, we were encouraged to team up with an existing organization that we won't name. But we were leery. We considered Birthright to be so complex that it would need its own administration to manage it. If it were folded into another entity, we feared its distinctiveness would get lost.

Even with all those liabilities, we almost went with that other organization because we figured that its objectives were similar enough to ours that we'd save ourselves a lot of start-up trouble by plugging into its structure. But in the end we decided not to. It certainly wouldn't be easy to start our own operation and develop it ourselves, but we would also have total control. We'd probably make mistakes, since no start-up lacks them, but at least they'd be our mistakes. So that's what we did, and it has worked out very well.

Initially we came to the opposite conclusion when we started the Gift of New York, the program we created after 9/11 to deliver some of the cultural bounty of the city to the families of those who died in the World Trade Center attack. In that case, in part because we knew this was a program that would last only a year and a half, we didn't want to staff up a brand-new organization. Initially we turned to a New York group that was already doing something similar for people with special needs. They'd been at it for thirty-five years, and it seemed like a perfect fit. We'd supply the tickets and venues for the families of victims, and they would basically be our ticket bureau.

Despite the seeming similarities in goals, this partnership never came to be. They said it was impossible to alter their software programs, adjust their procedures, shift their approach, or do any of the things needed to serve our audience. We offered them decent financial support to help them accommodate us. They countered with a request for so much more that it seemed to be their way of saying no. At that point, we said the same. So we went out on our own, and that proved to be a wise decision. It took only four staff members and scores of volunteers working out of a couple of donated hotel rooms. And the program was a spectacular success.

As these examples demonstrate, the decision of whether to buy it or make it yourself is rarely clear-cut. There are always arguments to be made on both sides. And in the end, it becomes one of those gut decisions that are akin to choosing a spouse. Partnerships at this level are complex and intimate and should not be entered into lightly. Essentially it comes down to the hassle factor: Is a partnership going to lighten your load, or weigh you down? If the former, go ahead, and if the latter, don't. When you are considering the far starker choice of deciding whether to simply write a check or go through the serious work of building a new organization on your own, the choice comes down to your objectives. Are you invested in this personally? Or are you just invested in this financially? The more personal the commitment is, the more seriously you should consider the prospect of building something new.

Michael Solomon and Vivek Tiwary

The idea for Musicians on Call, a thriving program designed to bring musicians into hospital rooms to play music for ill patients, came out of work for another nonprofit, the Kristen Ann Carr Fund, created to honor the memory of a young woman who died of sarcoma in 1993 at age twenty-three. Jeff's son, Michael, was Carr's boyfriend, and toward the end of her life, Kristen asked him and her family to create a program to "keep this from happening to other people." Kristen's family was well positioned to do that. Her mother, Barbara Carr, is the long-time co-manager of Bruce Springsteen, and he agreed to play a kickoff concert in Madison Square Garden to raise money for the fund. Barbara also persuaded Wynton Marsalis, another friend from the music business, to perform at the recreation center of a New York hospital.

Michael Solomon attended, and he was stunned by the healing power of live music in a hospital. Like Barbara, Solomon managed musicians, and he had a friend, Vivek Tiwary, who also did that as part of a broader effort in the entertainment business called the Tiwary Entertainment

Group. Both were in their late twenties, entrepreneurial, and had a personal connection (Solomon through his girlfriend and Tiwary through his mother, who had died of cancer a few years before).

The Wynton Marsalises and Bruce Springsteens of the world were tremendous assets, but Solomon wondered: "What if we just took some of the normal, everyday artists we were managing and brought *them* into the hospital? What sort of effect would that have?" He and Tiwary arranged for a little-known band to play in the recreation center of a large New York hospital. It went very well, and when the band was finished, a nurse approached Solomon and Tiwary to say that some patients had been too ill to attend the concert. Would the musicians mind playing in their rooms? Solomon and Tiwary checked with the musician and said it was fine, so this performer went to each of the rooms and performed.

"It was so magical!" exclaims Tiwary now. "You could feel the atmosphere lighten. You could see the patients start to laugh. You could see the tired, weary nurses start to smile. It was just such an amazingly positive experience."

The two men wrote a business plan that night. They named the new organization, Musicians on Call. "In every good hospital, there is a physician on call," explains Tiwary. "We thought there should be a musician on call too."

That was in 1999. By 2008, the program was operating in four eastern cities and had delivered music for over 120,000 patients. It has grown much larger than the Kristen Ann Carr Fund that fostered it, and Solomon now harbors what he calls "intergalactic goals" for the organization, pushing for a second 100,000 patients and then a third.

Musicians on Call has an annual operating budget of about $800,000 that goes primarily for a five-person staff, office space, and transportation for the musicians, who otherwise perform for free. The staff's major effort is to find and train the musicians. Not everyone has the touch to perform for the sick and the dying. The staff also makes all the arrangements with the musicians and the health care facilities, which now number over thirty.

As with the Kristen Ann Carr Fund, Musicians on Call relies on the founders' network of connections. It has been invaluable for Solomon to have a background in nonprofits, which taught him the basics of operations, and he has a lot of talent to draw on for his founders board. Grateful as they were for the contributions of Springsteen and Marsalis, Solomon and Tiwary have found that they can't depend too much on entertainment industry stars, most of whom already have their own causes. And the organization was nearly done in by the economic slowdown after 9/11, when they had to turn to their most loyal supporters through a series of cocktail party fundraisers to bridge the gap until prosperity returned to the city.

While Solomon and Tiwary have their own nearly scientific measures of success, they also tally it in the extraordinary stories of the patients who have been moved by the music: the youngster with leukemia who hadn't said a word for two months until the musicians came in, and then clapped and spoke joyfully about the music he'd just heard; the older patient dying of ovarian cancer who wanted to hear a song she used to play as a girl and then sang along when it was played for her. When the piece is over, Tiwary says, the music doesn't end. "You can walk down a hospital floor, and if you're attuned to it, you can tell that Musicians on Call has been there. The effect doesn't go away."

Both men find it a little odd to be philanthropists at such a young age. "Most people get their careers off the ground first," Solomon says. But now, ten years into it, they find themselves in the position of wise elders for others who want to try something similar. "The first thing I ask is, 'Why do you want to start your own?'" says Solomon. "Is what you want to do not already out there with another organization?" If there is, he advises, go work with it and save yourself a lot of trouble. But there is nothing else out there quite like Musicians on Call. As Solomon puts it, "It's the quality that distinguishes us from the other entities in our space." Even now that Musicians on Call is up and running, Solomon still puts in five or six hours out of a forty-hour workweek helping out with the organization. The demands of Tiwary's profit job are so great that he can't manage that much. "I'll admit I'm a little sad about that," he says.

Still, both men find that Musicians on Call restores their faith in the music they promote in their day jobs. "There's a real power to it that I sometimes forget," says Tiwary. "You know, I'm stressing out about how many people are going to buy this album, and I'll say, God, what does it really matter? And then I'll remember Musicians on

Call, and I'll go, okay, yes, right. Music *does* matter. Music really does matter. It reminds me why I got into this business in the first place. And there are days when that really keeps me going."

Nancy Lublin: Dress for Success

"I didn't have any intention of starting any cult when I came up with Dress for Success," says Nancy Lublin, founder of a nonprofit that provides professional clothes for needy job applicants on their first interviews. "My deepest desire was to start an entity that would survive beyond me." And that it has. Started with an unexpected five thousand dollars from the estate of her great-grandfather, it has gone "megaglobal," she says, with corporate sponsors ranging from CitiBank and Microsoft to Chantelle and Diane Von Furstenburg/Saks Fifth Avenue. It has more than eighty-five affiliates across the United States and around the world and an extraordinarily steady media presence, generating twenty-five hundred stories in all media in 2007. Since its inception in 1997, it has clothed 450,000 women for interviews that might lead to a first job.

And it all began with that check for five thousand dollars. "I was in law school at New York University, and I hated it," Lublin recalls, "and I came home one of those cold, rainy New York February days, and there was an envelope in my mailbox with the return address of a lawyer in Florida I'd never heard of. My first thought was,

91

'Someone's suing me.'" When she opened the envelope, gingerly, she found the check. It was from the estate of her great-grandfather, whom she'd always called Poppy Max. As she looked at the check, she wondered—should she pay off her credit card debt, take a vacation, or buy some shoes? She got into the elevator, and as it ascended to the sixth floor where she lived, the answer came to her.

Nancy had never felt ill-dressed for an interview, but she knew how it felt to lack the right clothes for a formal occasion, whether for Thanksgiving or a wedding, and she was sure that women who didn't have the right wardrobe would feel all wrong when interviewing for a job. That's what popped into her head. She'd use the check to start Dress for Success. She didn't have the name yet, but she had the concept. And it just felt right. When she got into her apartment, she called her grandfather, Poppy Max's son, and blurted out her plans for the money.

He thought she was crazy. "No, no, no," her grandfather shouted. "You should put it into the stock market."

She called her parents, and they agreed: she was out of her mind.

She stuck with law school, but added this other project, which proved far more educational. She did some field research, starting with a couple of nuns from Spanish Harlem who thought that hers was a brilliant idea. One said that a woman had showed up for a job interview wearing a Sergio Tacchini track suit. Since it was the most expensive garment she owned, she figured it had to be right. When the nuns heard about the check for five thousand dollars, they said to put it in CDs, so it would be safe—and it was—but it was also inaccessible for half a year. "So technically we had no money for six months when we started," Nancy says with a laugh. "But I guess that's what comes of taking financial advice from nuns." She put the two on her board all the same, and she financed the operation with a credit card.

With some help, she rounded up discarded clothing from the fine ladies of the Upper East Side and other fashionable parts of town. It made a mountain of black on her bedroom floor. "It was really shocking," Lublin says. "There was just so much stuff!" It made her realize that she was accidentally serving a "secondary need"—relieving wealthy women of last year's wardrobe for a good cause. For the primary need, she got in touch with the social service agencies that worked with the appropriate clientele—but insisted that her contact there volunteer with Dress for Success for a month to understand what it was all about. The volunteer pool swelled.

Once the clothing mountain neared her ceiling, Lublin realized she needed to find another space, and she secured a nearby loft for five hundred dollars a month. Still, there were problems. For one, the often heavy-set women who needed clothes were a radically different size from the thin socialites providing them. The average donor was a size eight, the average client a size twenty or more. "It was sometimes heartbreaking," says Nancy. To find the right clothes, she turned to large-size clothing companies for their discounts and remainders. When the Atkins diet caught on, sizes started to come down, but a lot of the donated clothes simply weren't right, regardless of size. Blue jeans.

A wedding dress. Baby clothes. Blankets. "Lots of times, people were just dumping stuff," Lublin says with some irritation. With some research, though, she was always able to find places that would be grateful. And when she did have appropriate sizes, she deployed a squad, "Personal Shoppers," to help the women pick what would be right for them.

Finding and keeping capable volunteers was a constant problem. One grim Thursday afternoon, her staff of Personal Shoppers was reduced to three: a refugee from Goldman Sachs who was recovering from a nervous breakdown, a gang-banger who commuted to Dress for Success from her halfway house after a prison stint, and a woman who'd been told by her priest that God would improve her fertility if she volunteered. "Any one of these three would be tough to manage," Lublin says. "But three?"

After her second year at NYU, Lublin said good-bye to the law to concentrate on Dress for Success full time. She had planned to run it "like a knitting circle," but it quickly became far more. She learned words like *business model* and *sustainability* and acted on the ideas behind them. "You don't need to know a lot about the not-for-profit sector, or about business management," she counsels. "Just get involved, and you can make a difference. You can leap right in."

After spending nearly a decade building up Dress for Success and establishing it as a global concern, she realized her time with the organization had come to a close. She had nothing left to achieve. So she shifted to another organization, Do Something, that encourages teenagers to get involved in nonprofit activities. It was a struggling organization—"a mess," says Lublin—and her job was to turn it around. After six months, she had Do Something operating in the black.

What lessons would she draw from her experience? "Just do it," she says. Just find a niche—if you can. "There are probably too many nonprofits right now. And if what you long to do is already being done, partner up. We may need new ideas, but we don't need new organizations."

CHAPTER 9

Working with a Nonprofit

LET'S ASSUME YOU HAVE DECIDED TO PARTNER with a preexisting nonprofit to do the work of feeding the hungry, housing the homeless, curing the sick, or performing any of the other hundreds of thousands of important activities they do. And it is important for donors to recognize how little hands-on control they have and how small a role they play. At the very least, any one donor is far outnumbered by the staff and board members. But there is an institutional history to consider too. Each nonprofit almost certainly was in existence long before the donor came along, developing traditions, instincts, and habits, and, with luck, it will keep on for long after. Even the simplest nonprofit is a complex organism, and often an inscrutable one, with its tangle of personalities and multiple constituencies. And that can leave a donor mystified.

Indeed, it is fair to say that the whole field is a bit of a muddle. Vast and sprawling, the loosely joined nonprofit industry is huge and omnipresent, employing one out of every ten members of the American workforce. But the work is so varied and often so difficult to describe that few people can easily explain what they do.

In banking, automobile manufacturing, and software engineering, for example, it's pretty clear what goes on, even behind the closed doors of a back room. Not so in your basic nonprofit. Society has somehow veiled its work. Since the news media rarely report on ordinary good works, any coverage usually involves crises or malfeasance. The United Way may be a familiar name, but what does it actually do? Or the Brookings Institution? Part of the reason for this state of affairs is that nonprofits rarely make anything, so their work is strangely abstract. Many promote ideas and innovations rather than actually provide person-to-person help. Some of the "employees" aren't paid, which is certainly unusual. And one size does not fit all. With some, the organizational structure can be staggeringly complex; high-tech national institutions like Massachusetts General Hospital employ thousands. Or they can be fairly simple: Mothers Against Drunk Driving started as a kitchen table operation. It could happen here, as the local Pop Warner league did, or way over there, as it did with an organic farming initiative in Indonesia.

Life in the Negative Economy

Yet nonprofits all have one thing in common: they do not operate for profit. A tautology, sure, but an important observation all the same, for the implications are vast. It means that these institutions stand apart from the capitalist structure that governs so much of life around the world. That is no small thing. They operate in the upside-down economy that is about giving, not taking, and about service, not profits, and their culture often has some of an other-worldly, ecclesiastical quality that goes along with such airy notions.

Nonprofits still participate in the capitalist system, of course. They need to purchase supplies and pay their salaried employees. And just like conventional businesses, they compete in the marketplace for customers, even if theirs are nonpaying. Financial failure results in bankruptcy and dissolution just as it does in the for-profit world. But largely free of capitalism, nonprofits must be staffed by cloistered monks as far as many people are concerned.

Nonprofits also mimic some of the activities of governments, as they too are primarily concerned with delivering services to those in need. But nonprofits are different from governments in one important respect: they are not accountable to any public electorate. This fosters a certain freedom, a nimbleness, that elected officials can only envy. Largely answerable only to themselves, nonprofits have more in common with monarchies or dictatorships than with any elected government. Still, even nonprofits are not entirely free. To the extent that they depend on public funds, as many do, they are subject to government regulations, and in most states, the attorney general is there to make sure they conform to them. With tax exemption comes an obligation of transparency and social responsibility. But there is no requirement of saintly perfection, selflessness, or vows of poverty, despite what some members of the public might think.

Nonprofits face a host of other constraints. Their funds are agonizingly limited. Able to offer only relatively meager salaries, they cannot always attract the most talented employees, or afford to fully train them, or keep them from straying to higher-paying jobs. They are vulnerable to market forces like the current downturn. And they are certainly not safe from acts of God or human folly either.

Partner Up

Nonprofits are the entities that donors turn to in order to make their vision a reality. Foundations do too. Ours does. Even megafoundations like the Bill and Melinda Gates Foundation do. Whether its their work in public education or malaria in Africa, Gates relies on existing organizations to make change on the ground. It's like the way corporations depend on suppliers. General Motors doesn't build its own steel plant but contracts out to Bethlehem Steel. And the relationship works best when it is mutually respectful, where Bethlehem Steel doesn't imagine itself getting ripped off by GM and vice versa. Better still, they might work together to help Bethlehem Steel produce just the right kind of steel for GM in exchange for, say, a guarantee that GM would purchase a certain number of metric tons.

Not long ago, we attended a preopening of a restaurant by a well-known restaurateur in New York City, and it reminded us of the need for partnerships in all realms of business. At the start of the evening, the restaurateur gave a talk in which he described his relationship with his various vendors: the maker of the tasty chèvre, the farm that raised the lamb, the grower of the organic vegetables. As he explained it, we realized he was describing relationships that had become partnerships in the best sense—symbiotic, dedicated, with each side working together to bring out the best in the other.

The truth, however, is that such partnerships are very hard to create. In nonprofits as in for-profits, as in every aspect of life, the average is the norm. The good is hard to find, and the really terrific is vanishingly rare. While this is a challenge in most realms of nonprofit work, it is a particular strain in projects that are likely to go on for years, if not decades. If you were to sponsor Parkinson's disease research or diabetes research, you may need to devote as much as forty years of effort. You'll need to pick the very best researchers at the outset, or you will have trouble down the road. Worse, you won't realize you have picked the wrong researchers *until* you hit trouble down the road.

What does a good donor-nonprofit partnership look like? At its best, it is symmetrical, meaning that one side does not look down at the other, each side has a voice in any decision, and the power is evenly distributed.

Several years ago we helped create an organization in Canada we'll call Canadiana to work on enhancing Canadians' awareness of their history and heritage. It was a spin-off of the foundation's own program, and even though we had handed it off, we still had a lot invested in its success. Canadiana did fine for five years, building on the principles of partnerships so effectively that it grew as the result of several mergers with organizations having complementary approaches to the same overall objective. But then it hit a wall. Primarily the problem was with the leadership. It went through two executive directors in three years and struggled through a financial crisis in which revenue tightened in part because of its expanded role and little capacity to bring funding partners along, recognizing that their view of Canadiana came through the telescope of their former relationships. Through it all, we remained involved as an active funder, and we kept in touch with the situation through a former colleague who sat on the board. Getting the unvarnished details from her, we could analyze the organization more dispassionately than the board leadership, which had so much invested in the appearance of success. The board lost their capacity to have a "balcony" view of the organization because of the loss of several key senior managers. We saw an organization that was ill, even though treatment was available.

The solution of the leadership of Canadiana was to ask Charles for more money. We saw that as a temporary fix at best, not a solution. The organization had a structural deficit, a steady leakage of money, that was driving it toward insolvency, and unless its leaders addressed that, no bailout was going to help them. Of course, the deeper problem was that its board did not have current leadership to provide a road map to health. They weren't sharing information with their constituencies in an even-handed way. Past officers were able to penetrate the organization, identify the needed repairs, and get them done only because they knew members of the board and were trusted. Although not all Canadiana's leaders and managers welcomed them in, they did find a better balance between the organization and its unmet needs. In addition, these moves restored the organization's solvency and enabled new management to focus on program development rather than crisis management.

This is the value of information sharing. The fact that a key board member had to slip us the truth does not change that; it affirms the point. If she hadn't let us know, both Canadiana and the Philanthropies' investment would be gone today. With it, Canadiana has survived, and our contribution has been put to better use.

But true symmetry can be hard to establish and discern. Because of the complexity of nonprofits, it may not immediately be clear to outsiders how well they are run or the special complications that they face. It's not just a question of transparency; it's not always clear on the inside either. Jeff had the experience of going to work at one nonprofit in a senior position and being told by the board chairman that he should immediately fire one of his subordinates whom he had soured on. As it happened, Jeff knew the staff member in question a little already and was not an admirer. But before he dropped the axe, he took the precaution of reviewing the man's personnel file—and there discovered that it contained a glowing recommendation from the very board chairman who had just recommended his firing. This emerged from the staffer's request that the chairman put a past compliment in writing. If Jeff had gone right ahead without checking, he might have exposed the organization to a serious wrongful-dismissal action.

Rather than let the man go, Jeff formally made him his direct report and set clear, rigorous goals for him to reach within six months. Only by establishing written, quantifiable goals could they determine the employee's contribution, or lack thereof. Sure enough, two months into it, the man quit, recognizing he was not up to the job. But the point of the story goes beyond how to resolve human resource issues or the autonomy of the chairperson versus staff. There is bound to be an asymmetry of information between a volunteer chairman and the paid staff. One wields considerable power but possesses shallow awareness; the other has fuller awareness but far less power. In this case, a staffer was able to cover a chairman by bringing his awareness to bear on a situation that was otherwise headed toward disaster. Nonprofits, beware.

A Partnership of Equals

For a donor, money does not buy everything. He needs to recognize that just because he has made a substantial contribution to the nonprofit, he does not own it. Most likely, he does not even know the nonprofit he imagines he owns. As public trusts, they are heavy responsibilities and difficult to run, even by full-time qualified professionals.

In nonprofits, there is an all-powerful triangle of three players—the donors, the board, and the senior professional staff—and the partnership is only as strong as its weakest member. When all three elements work well, the organization can soar. When one stumbles, the others are likely to falter too. If one becomes power crazed, the organization will go all out of whack. Ideally, this is a partnership of equals, marked by an easy flow of communication all around, a solid feeling of trust, and mutual respect. It's a give-and-take where no one partner is all give and no one partner is all take.

In our foundation, Jeff is the paid CEO, and Charles is the steward, who, with his board, oversees the funds he contributed. Despite the differences in their positions, each treats the other as an equal. For instance, ten years ago, Jeff did some work with an interfaith group on global development and the World Bank, and he reported back to Charles and his late wife, Andrea, about developments with the group. Jeff told them he'd be really interested in working on the project. He'd priced it out: it would cost seventy-five thousand dollars a year between travel expenses and outright grant money. Were they interested in his pursuing this? Charles replied, "I'm not interested, but you're my partner, and if you're interested, you should do it."

It was memorable because it revealed the fundamental mutual respect embedded in the partnership. Charles made it clear that he was personally not vested in the project, but he trusted Jeff enough to let him go ahead if he believed in it. This is the essence of parity: it's when you believe in your partner even when you disagree with him.

That said, although there can be these sorts of disagreements about day-to-day decisions, there has to be fundamental agreement on the essential strategic direction of the organization. If one of the players fails to share the nonprofit's worldview, that's a serious problem. Brilliant as any of the players may be, no one is going to change the mind of any of the others on something so fundamental. It's for this reason that whenever young professionals come in for counseling as they consider taking a job at a particular foundation, we encourage them to have serious conversations with representatives of the big three—donors, stewards, and senior staff—to find out precisely what they want to achieve. It is essential to know that up front. If you can't get behind it, seek a job elsewhere, for you will never convince them to alter their vision, nor they yours. And you don't want to build your professional life on such a fundamental disagreement.

That said, there is pressure on that central mission all the time. The disagreement can be philosophical in nature, but often it is financial, as a donor might offer a large sum of money to an organization if it'll broaden its focus a little bit. For example, a charity that is interested in helping red-winged eagles is offered a large sum from a new donor if it will expand its mission to include spotted owls. They're both large, endangered birds, and you could easily argue that to help the eagle is to help the owl, and vice versa. But the two issues are separate, and to combine them would dilute the core mission and cost the organization's quality of service, thereby decreasing the value of the donors' gifts.

So we say again to organizations: follow your mission; don't follow the money. If you follow the mission, money will come. If you follow the money, the mission can get lost somewhere behind you.

Zeroing In on the Fundamentals

In trying to decide which nonprofits with which to partner, a donor needs to conduct due diligence, just as with any other substantial business undertaking. The best way to go about that is by working outward in concentric circles.

Start with the innermost circle that involves the nonprofit's "true family": the chief executive, chief development officer, chief financial officer, and the other senior staff. Then turn to the board members, starting with the chairman. Look over the printed material and the Web site to review the accounts of who they are and what they are about. Make sure the descriptions and explanations are clear and make sense. Then do the drudge work of checking to make sure the organization's licensure or accreditation, where relevant, is in order. Check with the nonprofit rating services (Charity Navigator, Better Business Bureaus, and others.) If you find something untoward, use it to open a line of questioning. By itself, it may not be a reason to walk away. Also seek out neutral observers who can offer a candid evaluation.

It's a lot of work, but a substantial donation is a serious responsibility. The nonprofit is a potential marriage partner, really. And you would want to know the answers to questions that would help you determine if that marriage is likely to succeed. We'd ask:

- What are the distinctive features of the organization?
- Who's on its board?
- How often does the board meet?
- How serious is it about governance and oversight?
- Are the board members and senior executives trustworthy?
- What's the organization's history, and how well has it done?
- Is it self-reflective, or uncritical?
- Does it routinely evaluate itself?
- Are the leaders innovative and forward looking?
- Is its corporate culture comfortable—not too loose and not too tight?

One element in an organization to be wary of is the charismatic personality. Too often in the nonprofit world, an organization revolves around a star—sometimes the founder, sometimes not—as the solar system rotates around the sun. This celebrity is thought to be more important than any donor, staffer, or board member, and in our opinion, he and his ideas win too much attention, rarely receiving the scrutiny they should. Because of his stature, his ideas are, by definition, brilliant, and he seems to float above everyone unchallenged. The donor can't do too much about that, except to identify such an individual ahead of time—by checking with previous donors for their experiences—and to stay away if the celebrity personality seems to be a hazard to the organization, making it an ego trip or costing it its edge. The donor shouldn't go in thinking that he can bring the leader down, as more often than not, the charismatic personality can outlast any board members who might try to oust him.

A major donor should decide what role, if any, she wants to play in the organization before she makes her gift. In most cases, receiving reports will satisfy her. However, she may want more. It could be a seat on the board, and possibly on the executive committee, so she can monitor what happens with her gift. She must remember that when taking this position, her primary responsibility is to that organization, and not to her gift or pet project. Also, she may not want the hassle of getting so personally involved. It may be enough for her to monitor the board from afar, making sure that there are good people in place in the staff and on the board. Plus, it may be frustrating to be on a board she can't control, no matter how much money she has contributed. Or, if she does indeed have extra power because of her donation, the other board members might resent her for it.

If she chooses to use her donation as a door opener to joining the board, she could begin her campaign by doing some gentle politicking with her fellow board members over lunch or coffee or on the phone. Here, she has to rely on the strength of her ideas, not the amount of her gift. She needs to spell out what she can bring to the board and what she would like to see the organization do. If she wants to gain sway with her cash alone, she would be better off starting her own nonprofit. If she does get on the board, she'd be wise to forget that she ever made a contribution. If she's good, her gift won't matter. If she's bad, no gift will save her.

Jeff recalls a board where one of the major contributors was a complete pain. He'd raise his voice and pound the table in a vain attempt to put his points across. He thought his gifts gave him dispensation, but no. Although he was probably one of the largest donors on the board, he was never asked onto the executive committee, much to his frustration. Finally, he came in to see Jeff for a heart-to-heart. "I've given enormous sums of money, done everything asked of me, never missed a meeting," he complained. "How come no one takes me seriously?"

Jeff had to be straight with him: "Have you ever listened to yourself?"

To his credit, the man learned from that exchange, toned down the loutish behavior, and finally was promoted to the executive committee.

Every Donor Makes Mistakes

Here at the Philanthropies, we certainly do make mistakes. A big one, early on, occurred when Charles gave the foundation too much money. We got too big, too fast, and our ambitions outran our capacity to execute our plans. In this instance, flush with cash, we entered into a big program for Israel's thirtieth birthday anniversary called Independence and Interdependence. It was going to be a cultural extravaganza with dancers and singers and a vast orchestra, and it would start in Israel and then come to the United States and Canada. To pull it all off, we rounded up a number of gifted amateurs and took it on ourselves to shape their efforts into a show.

Disaster! The show never came together, and we had to abandon the effort at some cost. Our mistake? Although it sounds painfully obvious in retrospect, we didn't realize we weren't in the music business. We should have hired an impresario to create the show for us, subject to our approval, and let him collect all the performers. It was a classic case of donor hubris. Instead of hiring the nonprofit, we became the nonprofit. We forgot that we were just the donor.

We were in no position to start a show or to create anything, really. It's the peril of being rich—or, more to the point, of being perceived as rich. We were inclined to do everything ourselves so we wouldn't be ripped off by any subcontractors. Well, that is exactly backward. Any subcontractor knows far better than we do how to keep costs down and can keep vendors in line, and he is in a far better position to do that if his name, and not ours, is on the contract. If vendors are negotiating with us directly, they're going to think, *Bronfman is rich, so he'll pay extra.*

All relationships, whether in love or in business, are inherently tricky propositions, and the relationship between donor and nonprofit is no less so. Indeed, because nonprofits operate in this strange, largely uncharted realm of economic life, there are even more ways to err. But there are also ways to prosper. And this, in the end, is the reason for such scrutiny: to work all the angles to improve the chances for triumph. Because the challenges are great, the dedication must be greater still—which will only boost the satisfaction when you succeed.

The ACBP Approach

At the Philanthropies, we have an approach to taking on new issues that is worth describing. It consists of a series of discrete steps, each of which becomes a decision point: to continue or abandon. These steps are:

- *Needs assessment*: When we identify an area of interest, we try to fully understand the field and determine the degree to which there are unmet needs.
- *Idea generation:* In pure research, this would be the moment that the principal investigator forms the hypothesis. In service development or funding, we form our operating assumptions, including goals and objectives.
- *Research:* Before turning the idea into action, we do or contract for research to better understand the "market's" reaction to the hypothesis. This leads to a reassessment of the operating assumptions and the development of the next phase.
- *Demonstration phase:* With no more than one partner (too many cooks do indeed spoil the broth), we support or administer the risk capital phase of a new initiative. This is the moment when we try to be bold, welcome noble failure, and measure everything.
- *Go–no go:* Based on the findings of the measurements, we determine whether we are comfortable going to others for support of the idea. Analogous to new business development, this is the moment to go beyond the angel investors to those early adopters who provide mezzanine funding. It may also be the moment when we say that

we should not proceed, sunset the project, and simply make our experience and findings available to those who might learn from that experience.

- *Partnership development:* Here we become the enthusiastic salespeople seeking (and generally finding) others who can share the vision and lend their financial resources to the initiative's development and scaling.
- *Sustainability:* It is now time to help the initiative emerge toward independence, permanence, and growth through evolution into a solid, well-run nonprofit.
- *Get out of the way:* Founders and funders need to understand the importance of not standing in the way of the program's development.

CHAPTER 10

Running the Show

THE DIRECTOR, OR TRUSTEE, ON THE BOARD of a nonprofit is a uniquely American phenomenon who owes his existence to the neither-fish-nor-fowl peculiarity of the nonprofit itself. A nonprofit is, as we have said, neither a for-profit nor a governmental agency, although it shares some of the characteristics of both. It operates in the sweet space between markets and government. Because it exists beyond the reach of governmental control and market forces, the nonprofit needs a stabilizing, organizing principle all of its own. And that is the power invested in its board of trustees, which serves, in the engineering sense, as the organization's governor.

Placing Trust in Trustees

Trustees are almost miraculous beings. Even though they are drawn from ordinary walks of life, are usually untrained as to board service, and serve without pay, they have to be, and often are, repositories of wisdom and good judgment—citizen magistrates, really. Society has placed a lot of trust in them. Trustworthy herself, the trustee is also the keeper of a public trust. Since the nonprofit is, indirectly, supported by all the taxpayers by virtue of its tax-free status, the trustee's role is to make sure that it lives up to its obligations to the community it serves. She is also there to make sure the nonprofit survives into the future, if that makes sense, that is, the organization's mission remains relevant.

Although one thinks of trustees, too often, as white late-middle-aged men in suits, the range of trustees is as wide as America, with all races, ethnicities, sexual orientations, and income levels, as well as both genders, represented. This is so now more than ever before, as boards everywhere have made serious efforts to expand their diversity. Members represent varied constituencies, varied connections, and varied perspectives that are essential to expanding the board's awareness of the world around it.

Temperamentally, trustees run the gamut. Although it's been our experience that while qualities of intelligence, wisdom, and warmth are all highly prized, good humor is probably the indispensable personal characteristic, for board meetings, especially lengthy ones on difficult topics, can be a strain without a good joke or two. Plus, board work should not be serious business from end to end.

It is useful, of course, that boards have all the standard professional abilities—in accounting, legal, marketing, and so on. And inevitably, people of wealth and influence will take their positions, although ideally not all of them, around the table. Beyond that, the attribute that we have come to appreciate over any other is congeniality: the ability to partner with fellow board members, staff, and other organizations. This isn't just a matter of glad-handing, although that may be a part of it. It is more an openness, an ability to recognize the value of other potential contributors in a way that is sincere and winning. Partnerships are essential in this business, as they are in most other businesses.

Far more than corporate boards, nonprofit boards attract all sorts. But a principle of equality must hold, in external partnerships as in internal ones. There are no lead partners and junior partners. There are only partners. A common mistake of board members is to defer too much to the rich and powerful in the room. Don't.

You do them and the board no favors. Jeff once conducted a study of seven organizations that failed, either because they closed, were acquired, or they hit an existential crisis. He interviewed four board members of each one, and the single most common theme in all the interviews regarding the failures was an overreliance on the board chairman, making him all powerful. Other board members listened to him too uncritically, and they let him take on too many of the tasks that should have fallen to other trustees.

Our message is this: when you join a board, bring to it as much healthy skepticism and ask as many probing questions as you would in your day job. There is no less at stake. Too often, board members view the board as a club, where membership is their reward for their years in business, rather than as a sacred responsibility that requires no less attention than their "real" work. So they are less likely to ask the tough questions that yield the most revealing and important answers.

How to Be a Trustee—and How Not To

That said, it is never a good idea to ask the questions in a pushy or hostile way. "Why would you ever bother us with an array of such pointless data?" is not the best way to phrase an objection. But if the substance of the question, regardless of the phrasing, may cause some discomfort, board members can always inquire after the meeting in private or by e-mail. It doesn't matter where or how the question is asked. It matters only that it is asked—and answered.

That inclination not to make waves is sometimes pushed to ridiculous extremes in nonprofits, and it's unfortunate. This nice-nice ethic has led to something more pernicious, which is a need for universal agreement before making a move. On its surface, this is an appealing aspect of board life, as it suggests that everybody is getting along. But it is more likely to hamper initiatives, for it also means that boards may not be able to agree on the bolder projects—the ones that are inherently risky or controversial but could yield the most dramatic results. No one wants a board to degenerate into factionalism. But legislatures decide things by a majority, not unanimity, and they can tolerate large quantities of "no" votes without collapsing.

Still, in nonprofits, decisions that are made by just a few votes either way may well lead to bitterness on the losing side. In the spirit of consensus, we recommend a compromise of a supermajority, meaning that the bulk of the board, say two-thirds, needs to approve, but that a cluster of dissenters would also be welcome. Free to express their disagreement, they are also more likely to share their wisdom.

Here's an example. In 2008–2009, the country experienced a sharp economic reverse, causing some serious soul-searching on nonprofit boards all across America as they tried to decide how to respond to the fiscal crisis. In the face of declining revenues, the temptation is to cut expenditures across the board by a set amount, perhaps 20 percent. This is painful, certainly, but it is also equitable, and no one segment of operation can be said to be treated unfairly. For all these reasons, it is relatively easier to achieve consensus agreement from the board on that approach. Still, it may not be the smartest way to go. It may make more sense to take a surgical approach and, say, start a promising new program, shut down three underperforming divisions, cut back another one by 40 percent because its services were less essential, and continue everything else at the current budget. That may be healthier for the enterprise, but it is often harder for the board to come to such a complex and potentially divisive decision. Some members of the board might favor the so-called underperforming divisions;

others may consider some of the others even worse. The points of potential disagreement are many. We say, *Take them on.* Boards should not be so afraid of risking comity that they fail to live up to their larger fiduciary responsibilities. After all, the board's obligations aren't to the board; they are to the organization.

What's Expected of You

For all boards, the price of membership is fairly substantial, although it is a price that can be measured in any number of ways. First, it requires a duty of care and a duty of loyalty. While sitting at that board table, your only concern should be the interest of that organization. This is often challenging as you may be serving at that table because of your involvement in other organizations. Many boards expect financial contributions from their members, sometimes fairly steep ones, up to $10,000 and more. One medical center expects annual contributions of at least $100,000, plus seven-figure capital gifts. And board members are frequently expected to solicit as well to reach a combined "give-and-get" total. They also may be responsible for covering any shortfall in the budget. If the board has approved a budget of $1.2 million but only $1 million materializes in revenue, it's up to the board to fill the gap—or not approve the budget. That is the board's fiduciary responsibility, one that many members and potential members overlook.

Even beyond the monetary obligations, there are other contributions that board members need to bear in mind, ones that are possibly even more valuable. It might be for help in marketing, often a desperate need for nonprofits, which rarely can afford to pay an agency or hire their own staffer. Or it might be for help in training their middle managers, an essential activity for which they have little or no budget. Board members can size up the organization's needs for themselves and assess how they can provide them.

But inside the confines of the board, there is also a work component, which can be heavy. All boards are working boards. Strategy, marketing, outreach, finance: these are just some of the areas where board members might pitch in to plot strategy or provide advice. The workload is not necessarily light. Typically a board meets for several hours four or five times a year, and there are likely to be that many meetings of each committee beyond that. Committees often represent the place where the work of the board is carried out. Program committees determine the policies governing the agency's operations. They generally designate the areas of growth and expansion or contraction. Capital planning committees focus on the physical plants of the organization and oversee planning and expansion of the capital structure. Finance committees are charged with the oversight of the organization's budget on both operating and planning bases. While we too believe that camels can be horses designed by committee, an array of solid, well-functioning committees spreads the work of the board around, giving opportunities to identify good future board leadership in the process. On top of board attendance and committee assignments, there might well be dinners and events to attend.

Again, it is imperative that the board members know, believe in, and seek to advance the nonprofit's mission. Ideally this is part of a new member's orientation before joining. But it should work its way into every member's DNA, so that the member is not just a believer but a representative. Because nonprofits rarely have public relations firms to spread the good word about what they do, some of this work falls to the board members. You can't be a full keeper of the faith without being an evangelist. Members may not deliver the gospel to more than a few hundred people, but that doesn't matter if they are the right handful. Influential board members have influence. Here are two examples.

Charles has been on the board of the Mt. Sinai Medical Center in New York City for a few years now. When he first joined, the hospital was in financial extremis. Within a few years, it was turning a significant profit again, but the word had not gotten out. In social settings, when people heard he was on the board of the Mt. Sinai, they would invariably say, "Yes, terrible what is happening over there." And Charles would patiently correct them and cite the actual and most recent numbers, which he had just seen at a board meeting. This stark encounter with authoritative information can leave a powerful impression, and Charles found that it changed important minds, and he started to hear pessimistic assessments less and less.

When Jeff took over a troubled psychiatric rehabilitation agency in New York, he quickly realized that before he could change the agency, he had to change its image, and he'd have to start with the board. Dysfunctional as the agency was, the board was even worse. Members weren't showing up for meetings, and the average member age had risen alarmingly. How to turn this around? Jeff turned to a celebrity broadcaster who had once offered to return a favor: he asked her to join the board. Realizing the many demands on her time, he was clear about the commitment involved: she didn't have to attend committee meetings regularly, but he wanted to use her name on the masthead. She agreed. Then she happened to mention a friend who was the head of a major investment bank. He became interested and ended up contributing handsomely to the agency himself. And he encouraged other Wall Street executives to do the same, and many followed suit. What's more, when he learned that the agency was having trouble finding jobs for its rehabilitated clients, the friend called his personnel director and instructed him to hire one agency client per month. That's influence.

In this example, Jeff was a paid employee, not a board member. And that points to a curious truth about social connections. In seeking new board members, a board's own nominating committee is rarely able to reach up in terms of the holy triad of power, fame, and money; its nominating committees can only reach across or down. But as Jeff demonstrated, management is not constrained in that way; it can reach as high as it pleases. And this is important for troubled boards to realize. Although this is not the conventional wisdom, it is the fact: management can be very helpful in boosting the impact of new board members.

There is an internal aspect to this, too, as the board member needs to be vigilant in ensuring that the organization itself adheres to its mission and that new programs don't veer off message, or that paid staff lose track of the core purpose of the organization. The board should be the keel of the nonprofit, helping it hold its course.

Even more than tight agreement, the key to successful relationships around the boardroom table is simply a good rapport. There needs to be a balance of candor and comfort. Too much candor, and it's uncomfortable; too much comfort, and there is no candor. At most organizations, comfort wins out. That can lead to an information lockdown, and anything that is the least bit unpleasant never gets a hearing. But if you can achieve rapport, then every proposal and observation gets attention without fear of disagreement, and no one is frozen out.

It's the same with the relationship with paid staff. It too is a matter of rapport. You can tell at a glance which nonprofits are running well just by taking a look at the way the chairman of the board and the CEO interact. If it's loose and easy, everything is fine. That's no small achievement, for the relationship between the two, as between the board and paid staff generally, has many potential kinks. Essentially there is an asymmetry on virtually every level. Board members put in a fraction of the time of paid staff, so the staff is likely to know far more about key issues than the board, and, more perilous for the organization, have more time to influence critical decisions. Yet the board is theoretically in charge, setting the agency's direction and purpose. And there are contrasting demographics too. The organization is likely to be staffed by virtuous young people decades younger than the board members, and the staff's net worth, accordingly, is likely to be dwarfed by the board's. All of this can lead to some resentment if each side doesn't take steps to counter it. The tone is set by the chairman's attitude. If she is respectful to and appreciative of the staff, so will others be. And the same goes for the executive director on the other side. As we've said, nothing matters quite so much as the way the two treat each other at meetings. A relaxed joviality between them can preempt a lot of ill feeling.

Well-run boards are self-reflective and understand that they are stewards. They welcome term limits and the dynamism of new people and ideas that challenge the status quo. They are open about their responsibilities, including the evaluation of the chief executive, and they engage in self-evaluation as a board.

In general, a manner and a style can matter more than anything the chairman actually says. Leadership is much more a matter of nudging than it is of pushing, and what's nudged is usually the board. Nudges are so subtle they can sometimes be undetectable, but that doesn't mean they are ineffectual. And it's that combination of subtlety and effectiveness that we consider the hallmark of great leadership. You know a chair has done well if, when his term is done, the board believes that it alone is responsible for all the good results.

One last recommendation for board members: Be patient. Listen. And wait. Wait until others are finished before you present your point of view. Only then is your argument likely to tip the scales. It can be especially effective to reframe the debate in ways that are both fair and favorable to your point of view. You are revealing a consensus even as you advocate your position. It looks like wisdom, and it is.

Staff Secrets

If governance is on the board side of the equation, management is on the staff side. When you think of management, you tend to think of the illustrious Fortune 500 CEOs who are pictured in glossy business magazines. But nonprofit management is an entirely different beast. The CEO (of myth, at least) is a loner, a figure descended from the solo pioneer struggling to survive in hostile territory. The nonprofit manager, by contrast, is the successor to those historical religious figures, with roots in the communal, purposeful, and constrained religious order. The best of these managers are extremely discreet. Unlike Teddy Roosevelt's image of the presidency, these managers walk softly and carry no stick at all. Their success is measured not in dollars but in stakeholders. An expanding nonprofit is a healthy one. Ideally, by strengthening existing connections and partnering up for new ones, they reach out in ever-widening circles, expanding the reach of the organization they serve—and putting that organization on an ever-stronger footing, with ever-greater influence, in the process.

That's the quiet model, and it is the predominant one. But there is also a louder version, which you find among the leaders of large and prominent institutions like universities, hospitals, and museums. All of them have egos, and nearly all of them are public figures. But they too, in their own fashion, have built up their account in the favor bank with their stakeholders too. They do it by drawing on the considerable prestige of their institution, so much so that they become virtual stand-ins for it. When Harvard's president steps into a room, it's not just Drew Gilpin Faust making an appearance, but vaunted Harvard itself.

The business CEO has to worry about the bottom line. She has a board, analysts, investors, customers, employees, unions, and as many stakeholders as any nonprofit executive. The nonprofit CEO has his mind split in two. Half goes to management of the rather complex nonprofit operation, dealing with budgets and personnel and much more. The other half goes into making and demonstrating mission progress. Among the challenging elements for the nonprofit executive are some of the differences in structure and function. The public company board is typically small, includes senior management, and consists of financial stakeholders with a primary investment in the company. Financial measurements and benchmarks are omnipresent, enabling analysis against oneself over time and comparable firms. There are rewards for superior performance that benefit the capital structure of the company, as well as management and the shareholders, who fully understand their return on investment.

Contrast that to the nonprofit that operates with a larger board, the members of which may not have a serious involvement in the organization. While there has been progress in benchmarking, it continues to be in the dark ages, despite the fact that we are in an information age. There is little correlation between performance and growth, rewards, and, indeed, satisfaction, for it is often unmeasured and unacknowledged.

Ultimately, though, it is the stakeholders who demand attention, and there are competing ways to deal with them too. Some years ago, Jeff was being considered for the job of being chief operating officer at the New York United Jewish Appeal–Federation of Jewish Philanthropies, when that had recently been created in a thirteen-year merger process out of two organizations. Uncertain whether to take it, Jeff consulted a friend who was actively involved and said that the job was brutal, the second hardest job in New York (after the mayor's) and it would go one of two ways: either Jeff would do nothing and offend nobody and he could breeze through for twenty years and leave unscarred but unfulfilled, or he could do the job as it needed to be done, make the tough decisions, and have his head handed to him as he offended the stakeholders who empowered him in the first place. He took the job. That is the choice at most of these jobs: it's the choice of no choice at all. You can move the organization forward by leaving some key shareholders behind, or you can keep all the shareholders and be stymied.

In the midst of all this trouble, a manager needs one thing in quantity: a human touch. A delicacy, a sensitivity, a sense of when to soothe and when to cajole and when to roar. We have noticed a curious phenomenon in the hospital industry in New York. A disproportionate number of CEOs of major hospitals now come from a seemingly unlikely background. They're psychiatrists. It seems like something out of a Woody Allen movie, but it's true. And why? It's hard to say for sure, but we think the answer is because they, more than any other medical specialists, know people. They are attuned, they know how to listen, and they know how to speak with emotional precision so they can avoid the needless controversies that consume more thoughtless and more egotistical leaders.

And the discussion inevitably leads back to us at this midsized foundation. Charles is the chairman; Jeff is the paid CEO. How have we made it work? We almost didn't. Charles was initially convinced that Jeff, tall and imposing with his Beefeaters beard, was too standoffish for the role he had in mind. And Jeff wasn't sure he wanted to go into a "family business." But Charles reconsidered, saw the thoughtful leader he has discovered Jeff to be, and Jeff recognized that his initial resistance was due to a misreading of the principals. Jeff realized that he shared Charles's vision, and Charles recognized that Jeff would always tell him the truth.

So the partnership began, and although it is not flawless, it has created a strong organization in a challenging field for over twelve years. It has exceeded the sum of its parts, which is all we could have hoped for, and it has a vitality all of its own. It has that rapport based on mutual respect and an eagerness for each of us to help the other whatever the issue at hand. We always try to listen, and the listening is made easier by the fact that we share a dedication to the organization. There are differences between us, of course, many of them stemming from our different backgrounds. But we both love a good laugh and find a common cause in a world of tremendous importance to us both. We really like each other—what else can we say? We feel the joy.

CHAPTER 11

The Family

SEVERAL YEARS AGO, A WOMAN WE'LL CALL Jane arrived in our offices, very distraught. Her grandfather was a prominent real estate developer who had created a good piece of the New York City skyline before handing the business off to Jane's father. He had extended the real estate empire to much of the Northeast. Now Jane's brother had taken on the mantle; he had pushed the boundaries of the company throughout the United States and into parts of South America and Europe as well. All in all, it was a tremendous accomplishment for the three generations.

Jane had never been part of the family company, but it was a huge part of her family's life, and she strongly believed she should have a voice in it. Wanting to do something more meaningful with their wealth, she had convinced her grandfather, father, and brother to set up a family foundation and endow it with $50 million, a huge step. But then they couldn't agree on what it should do or how it should be run.

Jane persuaded the men to bring in a consulting firm to try to work all this out. But after more than four years of heated discussions, the family members had gotten nowhere. They couldn't even agree on which search firm to hire, let alone get started on choosing the executive director. They had used three search firms in the past two years, and Jane had little confidence the current one would last any longer than the previous ones.

A major problem was that all three heads of the family firm— grandfather, father, and son—each naturally assumed that he would take the leadership role in the foundation. The grandfather assumed that his seniority would prevail. The father considered that his father was too old for such responsibility. And the son figured that he was entitled to the position, since he ran the firm now and was in full executive mode. Each was determined to advance his own agenda and block the agendas of the others. That hadn't worked out too well, and now the three were barely speaking to each other.

Jane had never developed a professional career, choosing to volunteer in addition to her life as a stay-at-home mom. She was counting on the foundation to satisfy her desire for a professional position and also to unite the many relatives in her sprawling family around a cause.

But rather than bringing everyone together, the foundation was tearing everyone apart. Jane's siblings, their spouses, and their children were appalled at the acrimony—even as they started to form battle lines of their own. The younger members of the family decided the older ones were out of it; the older ones considered the younger ones upstarts. And the younger ones wanted to support global causes, while the older family members favored local ones.

On and on it went, the divisions far more apparent than the commonalities. Several times in her first meeting with us, Jane broke down and just sobbed with frustration and disappointment that things had turned out so badly. She wasn't sleeping well, had lost weight, and said her husband had put a ban on the word *foundation* in their conversations. That last part was supposed to be a joke, she assured us.

Every Family Foundation Is Unhappy in Its Own Way

For those involved in family philanthropy, aspects of Jane's story likely sound familiar. Family dynamics can be magnified by serious wealth, and as in Jane's family, for every donation contributed, that money is taken from the family business and hence "taken" from relatives, usually the children, who might otherwise have received it as a legacy.

What are called family foundations in fact are usually not started by families, but by individuals who would like to draw their families into the endeavor, a setup that can be a recipe for disaster when the family doesn't go along. Kelin E. Gersick, in his book *Generations of Giving*, examined twenty-nine family foundations in close detail and discovered that the wide majority of founders were over fifty, white males, and business owners, most frequently having started the business themselves; their politics ranged the spectrum, and they came from a wide variety of religious backgrounds. He identified their primary reasons for starting a foundation as, in declining order, "tax benefits," "philanthropic agenda," and "family closeness and legacy." (See Figures 11.1 and 11.2. Also see

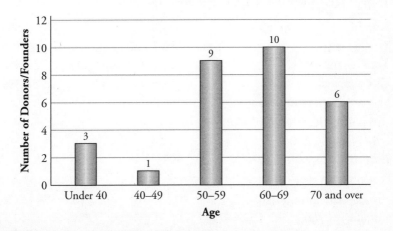

Figure 11.1. Age of Family Foundation Primary Donor or Founder

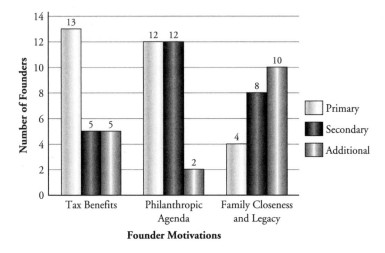

Figure 11.2. Founder Motivations for Starting the Foundation

SOURCE: K. E. Gersick, *Generations of Giving: Leadership and Continuity in Family Foundations* (Lanham, Md.: Lexington Books, 2004). Used with permission, National Center for Family Philanthropy.

Table 11.1 and Figures 11.3 and 11.4 for more general information on family foundations.)

Table 11.1. Snapshot: Family Foundations, 2006

Number of foundations	35,693	2.8%[a]
Total giving	$16,285,061,000	13.3%[a]
Total assets	$266,734, 900,000	14.4%[a]
Gift received	$17,658,257,000	38.3%[a]
Share of family foundations reporting less than $50,000 in giving in 2006	48%	
Estimated family foundation giving as a share of all independent foundation giving in 2006	59%	

[a]Change since 2005.

130

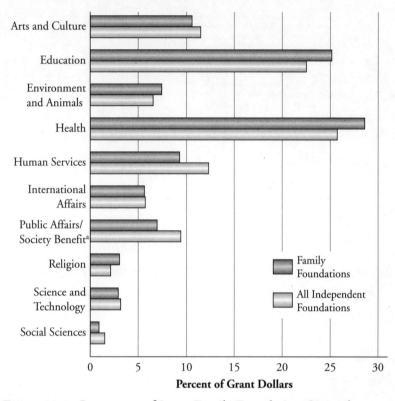

Figure 11.3. Percentage of Large Family Foundation Giving by Area, 2006

Note: Based on grants of $10,000 or more awarded by a sample of 956 larger independent foundations, including 577 family foundations.

[a]Includes civil rights and social action, community improvement and development, philanthropy and voluntarism, and public affairs.

SOURCE: *Key Facts on Family Foundations*, April 2008. Published by The Foundation Center.

In Jane's case, it was apparent that the family money was being dispensed, and it required family consensus to do it. But even in family foundations not tied to living donors or active businesses, no family ever thinks with one mind or speaks with one voice. As with Jane's family, every member of the family has a distinct

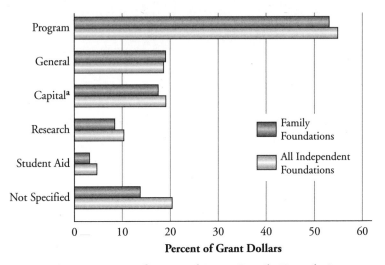

Figure 11.4. Percentage of Directed Large Family Foundation Giving, 2006

Note: Based on grants of $10,000 or more awarded by a sample of 956 larger independent foundations, including 577 family foundations.

[a]Capital support includes endowment funds.

SOURCE: *Key Facts on Family Foundations*, April 2008. Published by The Foundation Center.

perspective, one often made all the sharper by dint of sometimes painful personal history, which can make it difficult to fold into the common view. And unlike corporate boards of directors, family members carry in a lot of baggage.

So what do we do when we encounter a family like Jane's? First, we take off our philanthropic hats and put on our psychological ones. We're certainly not trained psychologists, but we try to move families from a hierarchical basis, with parents above children, and grandparents above parents, to a peer-to-peer one, in which everyone relates to everyone else as adults and peers. This is not an easy shift by any means. Other issues also require attention. The younger generation of twenty-somethings often feels disenfranchised by virtue of their age. Spouses feel excluded because the foundation follows bloodlines, not family lines. Women in the family who are not involved in the family business often feel as if they aren't being listened to. And so on. In our experience, none of these issues is inherently insurmountable. We have seen foundations come through more divisions and thrive. By their very nature, foundations are likely to have all the emotional complexity of families, but they can't overcome their issues by ignoring them.

We have a saying: Go slow to go fast. As with painting a house, so it is with operating a family foundation: preparation is everything. With Jane's family foundation, the preparation largely consists of addressing the family dynamics before the family foundation is established. Otherwise, the difficulties in play around the family dinner table will simply show up around the boardroom table.

Turning Hierarchy into Collegiality

Obviously, none of these generations is intrinsically any better than the others, no matter how passionately individual members may feel that their understanding of the world is the only legitimate one. And this is the crux of the issue: finding a way to recognize the value in each perspective without assigning primacy to any of them.

Instead of the old hierarchy model, we believe in a team approach where each generation offers unique skills to the team. Each new person on the board, and especially each new generation that comes on to the board, brings a new set of talents and the ability to translate their generation's needs. We're thinking of a Jewish family where the thirty-something granddaughter and her husband were adopting an Asian baby. The older generations assumed that despite the baby's Asian heritage, the family would maintain a Jewish identity. But the baby's background transformed the family into an Asian-Jewish family. So it is as all members of the post-boomer generations join the family foundation. Their presence redefines the family.

Generational dynamics aside, most families have tensions to confront. We encourage families not to avoid differences but to deal with them—sometimes by seeking outside counsel when necessary—in order to embrace both the family and philanthropy involved in the foundation.

If there is an emphasis on this being a family enterprise, then the board needs to involve any black sheep along with the white ones. But if the point is simply to dispense grants to certain predetermined causes, then the board can cut any black sheep out of the proceedings without misgivings. Again, the point is intentionality. Know what you want out of your foundation. Is it for the family? Or for the philanthropy? Know why you're giving, what you intend your legacy to be, and how to secure that, and the whole exercise becomes not just clearer but also more meaningful, even enjoyable.

If the point is to have everyone in the family involved in order to celebrate the unity of the different branches and generations, that would dictate inclusiveness and trump particular grants. If the founders recognize that certain family members have always gone their own way, that would dictate a more skewed structure to the organization. Neither is inherently better. It's simply a matter of determining which arrangement works better for the family in question.

Once a foundation is operating, if there are generational differences where the interests of the rising generation are different from those of the generation before, plan for that. If, for example, the elders of a foundation have always been major backers of the local Lighthouse for the Blind but their children want to shift to other causes, it makes sense that the foundation alert the

Lighthouse that the annual gift will gradually be decreasing or that it might make one last substantial gift to the endowment. This way, the transition occurs without being too disruptive to the Lighthouse, but the foundation can move on. Or the foundation could be structured so that the younger generations have their own discretionary funds or a distinct next-generation fund with which to pursue their own interests.

One Man's Experience

Charles has experienced firsthand his kids wanting to go off in a different direction philanthropically from his. His answer? Let them, and for his family, it has worked out brilliantly. His daughter, Ellen, and his son-in-law, Andrew Hauptman, brought City Year to Los Angeles; Andrew is on its national board. His son, Stephen, is on the board of the Suzuki Foundation in Canada, the largest environmental foundation in the country as well as emerging as a senior leader of the Montreal jewish community. Stephen's foundation is a leader in Montreal, doing important work in education, the arts, and the environment. There is no conflict between the past and the future in this family with this approach. When Charles and his son each used the values cards, three of their top five were the same: Leadership, Innovation, and Community. So their values are maintained from one generation to the next, even though the applications of those values might differ. This sort of continuity can be just as gratifying as the other kind, where different generations of a family stay together in the same foundation with the same objectives.

Those are the succeeding generations. What about the reigning ideology, or the founder's intentions that continue to govern the family—sometimes from the grave? While it may have become a family foundation, it is also the founder's money, and often he wants his intentions for that money to count long after he is gone. Those intentions may not be definitive, but they should at least be known. Don't assume succeeding generations know their parents' or grandparents' intentions. For this reason, we recommend that the founding donor record a videotape of himself expressing how he made the money and what he was hoping would be done with it. It's a good idea to play that recording for the board every year, so the founder's motivations remain in mind. We don't believe legacy should have a veto from the grave, but it should have a voice.

While some consultants recommend that family foundations decide from the beginning if they are going to be run on a hierarchical or egalitarian basis, we believe that's naive. Such a decision, if it can be made at all, comes only after a careful working out of the emotional issues; it can't be made on the spot. We know of one boomer, a CEO of a major company who, after a number of years of faithful service on the family foundation board, was told by his father that as a result of his service, he would be named president of this family foundation. Before he could declare his unadulterated pleasure, he was greeted with his father saying, "And I'll be the chairman of the board!" He was not joking. Nothing had changed.

That shows one of the issues that carries over from kitchen table to boardroom table: the relationship between parent and child. Ideally, we hope that will turn to a lateral one, peer-to-peer, but that will not happen quickly.

Follow the Money

Another difficulty can come from the money itself. To one member of the family, it is a point of guilt; to another, it is an opportunity to change the world. Some of the tension stems from the source of the fortune. In working through the issues that families encounter, we try to explore the legacy behind the fortune by finding out how the money had been made and what the founders' original intentions were for it.

It is important to remove the mystery. If the children don't know where the money came from, the news can come as a shock. In one case, an animal rights activist struggled with the knowledge that her family's business was a furrier. To the father, the company was a proud legacy, but the daughter didn't see it that way. By then, the older generation had jumped into discussions of what to do with the money before they had talked over what it might mean to the children to inherit responsibility for it.

Money is not just money. It is a legacy, and every legacy is a message passed from one generation to the next. Each generation has to determine for itself what that message might mean and how to square its understanding with that of its predecessors. We encourage families to pass down their life stories, lessons learned, and their values in addition to their financial resources. Their stories are often the most valuable legacy they can give their children and grandchildren.

It is one thing to get emotional ownership of the money and another to figure out how to spend it. One exercise we sometimes use to help with that is to pass out Monopoly money. We allow each family member to take a few thousand dollars, and it is always interesting to see what denominations they pick. If they take it all in five hundred dollar bills, it suggests that they are inclined to make a few major gifts. If they select smaller bills but more of them, we think they are more likely to want to sprinkle it around.

The Spouse

In family foundations, family members don't know what to do about spouses' unique conundrum. Are they in, or are they out? Many foundations impose a rule of consanguinity, limiting involvement to blood descendants and leaving spouses out of it. That can lead to bitterness and resentment, as spouses share everything in their marital lives except this. That feeling of exclusion may exacerbate an underlying issue stemming from a larger disparity of wealth. If a family is considering a foundation, chances are pretty good that it has other financial resources to pass down. That wealth is going to dwarf that of the spouse, which can lead to significant feelings of diminishment. And if spouses are included in a foundation, they can feel like equal participants or second-class citizens, depending on how they are treated at the board table. Since they are not descended directly from the founder, they can be intruders if they speak up, or they can feel like patsies if they don't.

In a frightening way, it also raises the specter of divorce, since that may seem to be the reason to leave spouses off the roster—and divorce, if it occurs, is indeed made all the more complicated if they are on it. Some couples will make a philanthropic provision for one or the other spouse to keep some money for his or her philanthropic ventures in case of divorce, just for this reason.

A Legacy to Hand Down

Ultimately the test of any foundation is how well it achieves inculcating its values to succeeding generations. By including Generations X and Y, foundations can serve a double function: introducing them to philanthropy and helping younger members become comfortable with the money that they are inheriting. It can be surprisingly traumatic to inherit a large sum of money, particularly if it comes out of the blue. When one woman we know was told by her parents at eighteen that she possessed a large trust fund and that she would be expected to handle it herself, she told us she felt disinherited, unloved. Why were they separating out this money for her? It seemed like a divestment. Another woman, on receiving her trust at twenty-one, gave it all away to nonprofits. This was her way of maintaining her independence. For the parents who make the money, the accumulation of a vast sum stokes their egos, but it can have a contrary effect on the heir who considers it something to live up to.

The Rising Generation

For young people involved or who will be involved in their family philanthropy, we facilitate a network called Grand Street (www.grandstreetnetwork.net). There are other venues for young people of wealth to explore their responsibilities and opportunities with peers, such as Resource Generation (www.resourcegeneration.org) and Leverage Alliance (www.leval.org). All the groups are peer networks that help connect young people with resources. They can swap stories on what it means to have this legacy, with access to money or philanthropy; what it's like to be solicited for a major donation at a young age; learning to say no; dealing with boyfriends or girlfriends around money. The Council on Foundations also has a next-generation group and provides guidance in how to be a productive member of a family foundation.

There are other ways of bringing a very young child into philanthropy. One technique we like is a moon jar with three coin slots, one labeled "spend," another "save," and a third "give." That, of course, is for the innocent phase of childhood before kids see the full financial picture. It doesn't take long before they do. Nowadays, children can gain an awareness of family money at a far earlier age than they did back in the era when heirs first learned of their inheritance at the reading of the will.

We have heard stories of teenagers using search engines to find out their family assets, all the more reason to start in on philanthropy early. For a sweet sixteen party, for example, instead of giving your daughter a car or lavish party, you could take a few thousand dollars and open up a donor-advised fund at your local community foundation in your daughter's name and then point her to one of the teen philanthropy groups in various parts of the country. It is also possible to place a teenager in an internship at a nearby philanthropic institution. You can have her shadow another family foundation to see how it works. Increasingly, colleges and universities are offering courses in philanthropy. (See Resource A for a list of some of the best of these academic programs.)

But whatever avenue a parent chooses, whether it is into a family foundation or not, she will end up introducing her children to the world of wealth. For obvious reasons, it is best to do this in a knowing fashion, the better to obtain the results she seeks. The child might indeed become a better philanthropist, but she will certainly become a happier and more balanced person.

CHAPTER 12

The Face in the Mirror

NO MAN IS A HERO TO HIS VALET, as the saying goes. And no donor is a pure unadulterated blessing to his grantee either. Pure as their motives might be and enlightened as they may consider themselves, donors have been known to toss an occasional spanner into the gears of a good, solid working relationship with the nonprofit they so generously support.

Usually it starts with a simple misunderstanding. The donor thinks he's spelled out one set of terms for his gift, and the grantee believes it involves another set. Because it was all done in a rush—last minute, under deadline, with little regard for technicalities—nobody stopped to write anything down. Needless to say, the donor prefers his "clear recollection." The grantee prefers hers. Typically the matter is discussed quite genially at first, but if the disagreement hardens into a solid dispute, the lawyers descend, the hostility mounts, and then both sides have a real problem on their hands.

In such a misunderstanding, there is plenty of blame to go around. It is rarely a matter of black versus white, and much more a case of gray versus gray, which is why the situation can become so intractable. Neither side is wholly wrong. One of the more famous disputes of this type involved a $20 million gift that Lee Bass, one of the legendary Basses from Fort Worth, Texas, made to his alma mater, Yale College, to fund an extensive course in Western civilization. Because of its scope, the course necessitated hiring some new professors. As the donor, Bass figured he should have something to say in the selection, and in particular, he wanted to be sure that the new professors weren't, in his opinion, too politically correct or liberal. Yale firmly believed that it was entitled to choose its own faculty without interference. After a tense four-year standoff, the conflict could not be resolved, and Yale returned the money—and not without some embarrassment to both sides, as both bore some responsibility that the gift had to be taken back so publicly.

The Foibles of the Donor Class

There are any number of explanations for a failure to communicate, but one is the power of money to bend even the most sensible people out of shape. Transfixed by the prospect of receiving a significant sum, the potential recipient may lose perspective in her eagerness for the money, and the donor may have his own anxieties about giving away a large portion of his holdings. After the deal has been struck, people tend to recall what they wish they'd agreed to, not what they actually did. In this collision of hope and ego, small issues can be magnified. Does the donor expect name recognition, and if so in what size letters, and where? Was this gift intended as one time only or an annual one? If the latter, will the donor give any notice before he terminates his giving? Will the gift be made in a series of payments, or one lump sum, or something in between? Will the donor receive a seat on the board? Will he be invited to all formal events?

Furthermore, when disputes arise and payment is halted, there is no built-in mechanism to resolve them. In business, if your

THE FACE IN THE MIRROR

biggest customer fails to pay on time, you can shoot off some increasingly sharp demand letters and then take him to court. Of course, you could do something similar to a nonpaying donor, and that would definitely get the message across and may win some money back. But it would also send chills down the spines of every other donor and potential donor that you've got, all of whom are thinking that if they pledge you money, they might be slapped with a lawsuit too.

The first rule for donors has to be no surprises. *No surprises.* None. As a donor, you have to be clear about your intentions and your obligations and stick to them. No less than on the for-profit side, your word is your bond. And to make sure that it is, grantees should record every pledge they receive. If you are putting on a cocktail party fundraiser, bring along a tape recorder to establish a record of exactly what the donor agreed to. If there is a substantial pledge, document it with a gift agreement, in as simple a format as possible. It dampens some of the party atmosphere but reduces more hurtful misunderstandings later on.

For How Much? What Did You Say? What?

We had an incident several years ago at a major fundraising reception we were hosting. Many of the New York financial heavyweights were there, including several major real estate players. Two of these men were very close friends and constantly challenged each other in the many ways that close friends tend to do. The fundraiser was very public, where people are called on in a certain order to announce their gifts in front of everyone. So we always made sure to call on the first of these two men, knowing that the second

---

would be challenged by what was likely to be a stretch gift. When his turn came, the first stood up and gave a charming speech about how earlier in his career, he was too poor to make a significant gift and, moved by the cause, had to borrow the money to make a respectable contribution. This time he was going to make up for that. Then, after a significant pause, he pledged *three million dollars.* Huge applause. Then his buddy got up and shyly mumbled a comment of his own and sat down. And we were utterly mystified. *What did he say?*

So we went back to the tape, and we played it twice, and it was absolutely clear that he had said, "Same." We acknowledged him for that amount. And he paid it. And we were really glad we had brought the tape recorder. Without the tape, the situation might not have ended so happily. A thousand people might testify he said $3 million, but if the market plunged or he turned sick by the time we asked him for the cash, he might have reneged.

And what if a donor doesn't pay? That's tricky. We recommend that the nonprofit management not handle it. The matter should be handled by his peers. They may have to renegotiate because of changed circumstances. But people give to people. It is an intimate exchange and should be treated with sensitivity and respect. Too many organizations treat their donors like ATMs and bang on them when they don't spit out the money. Don't. Donors aren't "prospects" or "cards." They are some of the most precious people in the organization. If they must be invoiced, never do so without reminding them how their hard-earned funds will be used.

Oh, and One Other Thing

There was an incident in Israel where a major donor offered $25 million for a major museum. The museum was over-joyed, the press went wild, and everyone in Tel Aviv was thrilled. Except for one thing: unknown to the public, the donor had made an agreement to replace the museum's name with his own. In Israel, there is no less ambivalence about wealth, power, and public recognition than there is in the United States. When the news broke, the uproar was extraordinary, and it left the museum with a Category Five public relations disaster. The widespread perception was that a precious public asset was for sale. Not good. The museum reconsidered its offer, the donor withdrew his gift, and the museum maintained its name.

Tight with a Buck

Some donors are known to play fast and loose with their pledges. We knew a man in New York who annually pledged thirty or forty thousand dollars, but by the end of the year, the cash was never forthcoming. When a volunteer followed up, he would negotiate it down to a much lower amount, like ten thousand dollars. That shouldn't happen more than once, but it happened repeatedly: the donor wanted to join the upper echelons, and the canvasser was happy to be the one who placed him there, then left collecting the cash to others. Although that behavior is extreme and a rare exception, things do change, and occasionally some donors can't honor their pledges for legitimate reasons having to do with illness, a business reverse, or other problems. In any other business, it would be called shrinkage and be considered normal. For nonprofits, it generally runs 3 percent or less. It's worrisome only when it jumps above that.

While almost all donors do pay, many of them pay at the last possible minute. A disproportionate percentage of all donations arrive in December, which is pretty late in the game to help a nonprofit's annual budget. While formal pledges can and have been used as collateral to secure loans, nonprofits take serious risk—and incur interest costs—in so doing. From the nonprofit's point of view, there are four rules to follow regarding donations:

1. Give until it hurts.
2. Make good on your pledge.
3. Do it soon.
4. And if you can't, do it on an agreed-on schedule.

Gifts That Keep on Taking

Donors tend to imagine that grantees care about only one thing. And they do care about that, but they also are interested in in-kind contributions. The lawyer who can contribute her legal skills, the accountant who can review the books, and the other voluntary acts of generosity we mentioned before all have value. But sometimes these donations are offered with conditions that make them considerably less generous. At the extreme, these are the gifts that keep on taking. Consider two examples.

The first is about a powerful corporate executive we'll call Marian, the major donor to a children's agency. One year she was to be honored at the agency's annual banquet. As it happened, Marian worked at a large company with its own outside public relations people, and she offered them to provide publicity for the event. The delighted executive director said fine, anything. Actually the event didn't need PR, but to prove themselves to Marian, the team swarmed all over it, drawing the executive director into hours of pointless meetings and then commandeering the nonprofit's overworked staff to execute the elaborate plan the PR people came up with. The moment the event was over, the nonprofit severed ties with the PR agency, which had become a drain on resources. The whole exercise had been a nuisance, but once it got going, the nonprofit couldn't stop it. The lesson? A nonprofit doesn't have to accept something because it's free, and it shouldn't assume that because it's free, it has to be valuable.

The second example shows how far afield some of these contingencies can run. We were once cultivating a donor for Birthright Israel, and it gradually became apparent that his donation would come with a sweetener for Charles in the person of the donor's niece, whom he was hoping that Charles would date. The expectation wasn't apparent until after the niece showed up at the strangest places, including the donor's home where we had been invited for breakfast very early one morning. No sparks flew, the niece returned home, and her uncle, the potential donor, was never heard from again.

Some donors ask for favors all the time — to use their bank, their accountant, their realtor for example. With a major seven-figure donor, this might be hard to decline, but such a donor is usually too sophisticated to pull such a stunt. Midlevel donors sometimes ask an innocent-sounding question, like why a particular accounting firm does the books when they know somebody else who does it much better for less. It may seem to be just a matter of information gathering, but there is a proposition inside, and the nonprofit has to be wary of such entanglements. Much of the time, such a solicitation is made out of the legitimate belief that the grantee can do better. But such inside offers can be risky too. The 2008 Bernard Madoff scandal, which caught a frightening number of foundations and public charities in the web of his Ponzi scheme, is perhaps the most prominent and far-reaching example of this. Social prominence must never obviate solid due diligence. Boards of directors can and must insulate the organizations from such social pressure, for it can steer the nonprofit's business away from a company in which the donor has an interest but which provides no special value to the nonprofit. No nonprofit wants to get caught in a conflict of interest. Reputations are far harder to win than they are to lose.

Donors, however well meaning, can also be guilty of meddling. They imagine that because they are helping to fund an organization, they are entitled to offer endless advice on how to run it too. They may want to be involved in personnel decisions, in matters of programming, in questions about where to expand. As we like to say: NIFO—noses in, fingers out. Donors can have all the information they want, absolutely, but no control. That sits with the board, as well it should.

That's especially important in hiring. The first rule of human resources is that the person who did the hiring should also be able to do the firing, if firing ends up being called for. So it is all the more important to keep any donor away from hiring decisions, lest he then be empowered to fire as well. Then you'd have a *really* intrusive donor on your hands.

The reason that nonprofits have to be so vigilant about outside influence, especially in personnel matters, is that people are pretty much all they have. There are no huge manufacturing plants, no extensive inventory. Each organization rises or falls depending on the people in it. Without the money to motivate their employees, nonprofits depend on a sense of purpose, a feeling of security, and a pleasant atmosphere to inspire them. Nothing could wreck all that more quickly than the discovery that a fellow staff member had been axed on the whim of a donor.

For their part, donors need to recognize that without a contented and productive staff, they are never going to achieve the objectives they sought to accomplish with their gifts. Indeed, if they can motivate the staff with their gift, they increase its value.

Money for everyone is protean, holding many meanings and many forms. But for the wealthy, it can be mistaken for power—power to be taken seriously and used to get their way. And some of that does occur. Like the proverbial man who's won the lottery, the rich might also think their jokes are funnier than most other people's and their observations more sage. People do flatter the wealthy, inflating their egos, and distorting their sense of their place in the world, in hopes of obtaining some of that wealth for themselves. While it's obviously counterproductive for donors to deploy some of the power of money by abusing the staff, there can be some perverse satisfaction in knowing they can.

It's too bad that many nonprofits, perpetually hungry for funds, are obliged to operate in the realm of the wealthy. It means that the nonprofit operates in two worlds simultaneously: the regular world they know and the world of wealth they can only guess at. The combination can be corrupting as nonprofit executives ride along on the ego trip of the wealthy, expecting box seats at the opera and first-class air travel. If those executives aren't careful, this can only widen the divide between the haves and the have-lesses, as they can lose track of the audience they serve in their desire to join the ranks of the donors they cater to. And that leaves nonprofits in a place they'd just as soon not be: one of the more class-conscious entities in America. The ranks of too many nonprofits have a tragic upstairs/downstairs quality, by which the staffers downstairs dream of life above and the donors above neither know nor care to know about life below.

CHAPTER 13

Philanthropy in Hard Times

IN THE FALL OF 2008, THE U.S. ECONOMY—indeed, the world economy—entered a downturn worse than any other in decades. Wall Street was decimated, the automobile industry imperiled, housing prices dropped, and stocks plunged. With incomes, assets, and confidence all down so precipitously, it made for the beginning of a difficult time for philanthropy. At such a time, demand for everything from food pantries and homeless shelters to psychological clinics and legal aid is enormous, at the same time that the funds to provide them are hard to find.

Economists have worked out the grim calculation: for every percentage point increase in unemployment, there is a disproportionate increase in state hospital admissions, another in heart attacks, yet another in use of emergency rooms, suicides, and too many other indicators of frightful distress. And states that might be asked to take up the slack have found their own capacities reduced. In most industries, the greater the demand, the more resources are mobilized to generate the goods and services to meet that demand. On the nonprofit side, it doesn't work that way: the greater the demand, the fewer the resources, and the more the supply shrinks.

Persistent Generosity

In the recessions of 1991 and 2002, Americans responded to such calamities by increasing their donations from the year before, a remarkable testament to their generosity. In 1991, with a 7 percent reduction in the Standard and Poor (S&P) index, there was a 3 percent increase in giving. In 2002, with a 17 percent drop in the Dow Jones index and a 23 percent drop in the S&P, giving increased by 1 percent. (Much of the outpouring of generosity after 9/11 had come the previous year, in 2001.) But in this most recent case, there has proved to be a limit to how much Americans can do. In the previous recessions, significant sectors escaped the damage. In 1991, real estate was dragged down, but Silicon Valley prospered. Ten years later, it was the other way around. While the dot-coms were imploding, real estate prices rose, enabling developers to amass tremendous fortunes. For this most recent recession, no domestic sector has been immune, and no country either. This has distressed individual stock accounts like few other events in the past half-century. Since close to three-quarters of giving comes from individuals, the broader economic impact of this period is likely to be ruinous on philanthropy. Indeed, late in 2008, Moody's Economics predicted a $110 billion loss in giving through 2010.

That can also provide some guidance for the nonprofit sector. Although demand does not by itself draw supply, that does not mean that it can't guide the nonprofit's response to the crisis. How should a nonprofit manage? The first rule must be this: no denial. Bad economic news needs to be faced directly and quickly. The second rule is: be flexible. Shift to where the funding is. Say you're with a family service agency, and you have always focused on counseling families and paid little heed to the needs of the unemployed. Now might be the time to shift your emphasis to job seekers, especially given that the government will be putting a lot of money into job retraining, counseling, and guidance. Nonprofits might consider combining with another organization doing similar work to achieve some cost savings by sharing back office staff and information technology.

The perfect storm metaphor is haunting nonprofits. It is truly a quadrifecta:

1. Donor discretionary income is down.
2. Foundation resources are down.
3. Nonprofit resources and endowments are down.
4. Government is cutting support to the sector despite stimulus legislation.

The great incentives for philanthropy in normal times diminish dramatically in bad times. During such hard times, boards need to be especially conscientious. None of these decisions are easy, and many can be fateful. Board meetings should not be conducted in a spirit of business as usual. Probing questions and revised management operational plans should be the new normal. Besides dealing with questions about the structure of the organization, the board will need to address the brutal economics of the situation. Better to face reality, no matter how brutal, than to cling to hopes that are indistinguishable from fantasies. The board should address itself to some central questions: If the nonprofit has an endowment, how should it use those funds to survive the crisis? As a rainy day fund to be drawn down to cover the shortfall, or as capital to be preserved? This is a tough call. Traditionally the nonprofit had drawn off the interest and shaved a few percentage points off the growth to balance the budget. But there is no growth now, only loss. Can the nonprofit still turn to the endowment to make the budget?

This is a time for both funders and grantees to seek opportunities for transformation. Can efficiencies be gained by combining administrative functions with other organizations? Would it be more efficient for a small foundation to make the transition into a donor-advised fund? Only by confronting such difficult issues can the nonprofit hope to weather the economic storm.

Madoff and Ponzi and Prudence

As if the economic crisis was not bad enough, 2008 and 2009 also delivered the Madoff scandal, the massive Ponzi scheme perpetrated by Bernard Madoff. It hit many nonprofit organizations, most of them trebly: their donors lost great sums and so were less able to provide support, a number of foundations supporting a broad range of nonprofits lost their operating capital and had to cut back or close down completely, and scores of nonprofits themselves lost large portions of their endowment and huge sums of operating capital that had been invested with Madoff.

The lesson for boards is, once again, to do due diligence. Just as no one is above the law, no one is above the suspicion of lawlessness. And that is as true of Bernie Madoff as it is of the many figures of supposed probity he co-opted. Upon closer examination of the funds, which ACBP did when we were approached to invest with Madoff, it became clear that his investments broke five basic, prudent rules:

1. When something looks too good to be true, it usually is. His returns defied reason and ignored market conditions.
2. The annual results are likely to fluctuate. Nothing ever goes up every year.

3. Investment firms should be an open book. Madoff's firm had no transparency.
4. No one had heard of the firm's auditors. A serious investment house hires serious auditors, or no one will take it seriously. Or should.
5. Trades were not independently cleared or custodial.

Prudence is the watchword with nonprofit investment policy. It is about wealth preservation, and much less about growth. Word-of-mouth and social connections cannot replace proper investigation and tough questions. If a nonprofit loses large sums of money, closing is usually the only alternative. So nonprofits need to err only on the safe side, performing a stringent risk-benefit analysis of any investment in which risk is exhaustively assessed. And to secure that, they should diversify.

In a time of such widespread financial distress, the organization's leaders need to concentrate on canvassing their donor pool. Most nonprofits depend heavily on a few major donors to provide the bulk of support. If this is the case, it behooves the nonprofit to get in touch with these donors to find out their plans. If one major gift drops out of the mix, the organization's budget can be thrown completely out of whack. If that is going to happen, knowing it soon is better than finding out later. (Smaller contributions are likely to shrink by 10 percent, but that is a much smaller portion of the total.) Concentrate on the major donors, who won't be offended and are virtually the only ones in a position to make a downturn much easier to bear.

PART THREE

The Gift

"How do I know you're not going to turn around and spend it on eggnog?"

CHAPTER 14

A Glossary of Gifts

LET'S ASSUME YOU HAVE DECIDED on the field you wish to support, selected the individual organization, worked out the partnership arrangements, and are ready at last for the magic moment when you write out a check. Well, before you do, wait. You have one last decision to make, and it is no less important than any of the others: What kind of gift?

You might think that, as Gertrude Stein might have put it, a gift is a gift is a gift. But there are many types of gift, depending on your objective and how much control you want to retain, and all have different implications. There is, in fact, such a panoply that the most efficient way to present this information is as a list. So what follows is the full roster of possible gifts, and you would be forgiven if you didn't want to wade through all of them. Feel free to skim this chapter to see the many varieties of gift there are and then zero in on the type, or types, of gift that concern you most.

Unrestricted Gifts

Let's start with the most basic gift of all: the straight-out hand-off of funds that the organization can do with as it wants, whether it's to add to the endowment, acquire land, raise salaries, or improve the air-conditioning system. This is called an unrestricted gift, and it is so eagerly sought after by fundraisers, and so deeply appreciated by recipients, that you should not be surprised if the president of the organization dropped to her knees in gratitude. From the recipient's point of view, unrestricted gifts are wonderfully versatile because they can be used for any purpose the administration has in mind, from addressing a sudden emergency to a long-term goal, and anything in between. It is the institutional equivalent of a blank check.

More broadly, an unrestricted gift is a testament to the donor's faith in the institution—chiefly, that it won't do something stupid with his money. Such gifts harken back to a time when donors unconditionally trusted the judgment of the leadership of the charities they supported and were confident that the leadership knew better than the donor how to put her money to the best use. Fewer people think that now.

Restricted Gifts

In the Newtonian physics of philanthropy, the decline in unrestricted gifts has led to a rise in restricted gifts. They are controlled not by recipients but by the donors, who expect nonprofit institutions to support their vision. The donors are the drivers, the organizations the cars. Here are some of the more notable types.

The One-Time Capital Gift
Of these restricted gifts, the most basic type is the one-time capital gift, usually given to an institution's capital campaign to raise money for something solid, like building new facilities or upgrading old ones. A capital gift, especially a one-time one, is restricted exclusively to such a purpose.

"And Not One Penny for Overhead!"

How we hate to hear that—and yet we often do. Although we commend donors for taking charge of their gifts, we regret that they often push that effort to this extreme. If donors won't pay for overhead, who will? How else are programs to be administered, and by whom, in what office space, with what technology and support staff? The no-overhead policy is very shortsighted. Although overhead certainly shouldn't take up the bulk of any gift, it can't be expected to consume none of it either. Our rule of thumb is that if we are going to trust an organization with our funds, we will also trust its leadership to be prudent in managing its overhead costs. How would you like it if you were not allowed to spend a penny of your salary on housing or utilities? Overhead is the cost to institutions of staying alive. Increasingly, boards of directors are responding to the "overhead concerns" of donors by devoting their own contributions to the overhead that the donors are so disinclined to fund, which may not be the best allocation of their support.

Yet these same overhead-averse donors sometimes turn a blind eye to the needless expenses that they themselves cost the organization. Not long ago, a new foundation was offering to support a social services program, but its executive director made it clear that the foundation would not give any money for overhead. The foundation Request for Proposals was so dense and elaborate that the cost to respond to it approached fifteen thousand dollars in order to deliver the detailed information required. There was a good chance that nothing would come of it. We had to wonder: Wasn't that even more wasteful than money spent on overhead? Foundations that are using Requests for Proposals and regular reporting should instead turn to standardized protocols and make the effort to get funding partners to do the same. It is criminally wasteful that strapped nonprofits must waste precious resources on duplicative reporting.

The Gift to the President's Fund

Some universities get around donors' aversion to unrestricted gifts by setting up a president's fund whose benefactions have all the qualities of an unrestricted gift but lack the name. Essentially this arrangement allows the donor to give to a fund that is controlled solely by the president, who can then use the money for any purpose she deems worthwhile. Again, this makes sense only if the donor has confidence in the administration. But then, he should consider making donations only to institutions whose leadership he trusts long term, for the president's fund is run not just by this president, but by the next one and all her successors as well.

The Restricted Gift for Program

Now let's turn back once more to the unrestricted gift's alter ego, the restricted gift, and consider it in a different context: the restricted gift for program, usually a single program. That makes it a bit more problematic. This is purposeful giving, but it is also a gift with a string or two attached, and we have been entangled by too many of them not to be wary. To the donor, it makes a lot of sense to restrict his gift exclusively to his own objectives—promoting swimming at the local YMCA, for instance. The donor swam at his local Y for years, loved it, and wants to see that swimming is always available there. This is all very good in theory, but what if, a few years down the road, the local Y's swimming program is in great shape, with a state-of-the-art pool and well-funded swim teams and instructors, when suddenly there is a serious shortfall in the Y's operating budget? It would be nice to be able to use the extra swimming money to avoid drastic cutbacks. And even if the needs are not dire, it might be good to be able to follow the spirit of the gift by using the money for, say, an updated YMCA brochure in which the swimming facilities are advertised along with the rest of the programs, or for repaving the parking lot, whose spaces swimmers sometimes use.

There is likely always to be an aspect a donor favors above all the others, and he should feel free to support that alone—but be aware that such a gift has its drawbacks as well.

The Restricted Capital Gift

Where bricks and mortar are involved, it's a restricted capital gift. Such gifts need not literally be confined to bricks and mortar, though. To commemorate his son's bar mitzvah, Jeff anonymously gave a pair of maple trees to plant in front of the synagogue his family attended in New York. Admired as they were by the congregation, they were beloved by his son, a thirteen-year-old who was especially moved by parental lessons that weren't spoken. A capital gift might be unrestricted, too, if it is made to a capital campaign that was open-ended and allowed to go toward any purpose the institution chose. Such a gift can be especially welcome at the latter stages of a capital campaign, after that first burst of enthusiasm has passed.

A Story of Smart Philanthropy

For years, the Kresge Foundation has addressed an aspect of nonprofit life that is of critical importance to the organizations but rarely gets any attention from donors: the final stage of any capital campaign, when donations often flag well before the ultimate goal is reached. Kresge's mission is to do this essential but little-recognized work by offering a hefty challenge grant to finish up the campaign and increase the rolls of donors in the process. Wonderfully idiosyncratic, the foundation wants recognition for its efforts but doesn't care what form it takes. As a result, there are now a number of institutional water treatment facilities with the name Kresge on them—so many, in fact, that some people may think that Kresge is in the water treatment business.

The Catastrophe-Related Restricted Gift

Aside from restricted gifts that the donor might dream up, many more have been generated by cataclysmic events like natural disasters. In the aftermath of Hurricane Katrina, dozens of funds were established by the Red Cross and other relief organizations for people wanting to help. These are catastrophe-related restricted gifts.

A Time-Restricted Gift

Donors who wish to support only one particular program might provide a program-restricted gift. A version of that is a time-restricted gift, limited to a specific interval—one year, five years, perhaps even ten years. Organizations like such gifts because they ensure funding for that entire period, permitting the organization to plan better. Such gifts reduce overhead since they mean that much less financial development, itself a cost. And a deadline can speed results.

A Point We Can't Resist Adding

Many donated elements remain unnamed because other donors are not like the Kresge Foundation and would rather not have their name on some unimpressive piece of equipment. One notable exception can be found above the urinals in the men's room at a major cultural institution where there is indeed a commemorative plaque—honoring the donor's brother!

The Challenge Grant

The challenge grant, like the one that Kresge offers, is a widely employed device that will (usually) double any other donations that come in during a certain time frame and thus serves to encourage other donors to step up. Insiders should consider ways to encourage less involved persons to give. The challenge grant is a tried-and-true approach.

The Virtual Endowment

One other restricted gift is relatively novel, and we have seen few instances of it but expect to see more. A virtual endowment, like an actual endowment, generates a certain "total return," frequently 5 percent, for the recipient institution. But the assets are not controlled by that institution; rather, they remain in the donor's portfolio—hence, the idea that they are virtual. They remain in the donor's possession during his lifetime and can be revoked at any time until his death, when they transfer to the recipient.

The Capital Campaign: A Better Kind of Pyramid Scheme

Capital gifts are rarely made in a vacuum. Most often, they are the product of a capital campaign that is run, in the best cases, like a military campaign. Consultants are hired to scour the landscape for potential donors and determine whether there are enough at the necessary levels to fill out "the pyramid," by which a large gift stands atop smaller ones. Typically for a $10 million campaign, a crowning gift of $4 million would be placed at the apex; three gifts of $1 million each would go in the next row, four gifts of $250,000 would go below that, ten gifts of $100,000 below that, and forty gifts of $25,000 would run along the bottom.

The fundraising team needs to know well in advance who can deliver these sums, and the board plays a key role here. Its members have been selected for their resources, interest, and financial contacts, and the board is itself a prime target. But there are still other prime candidates, which the fundraiser works up in a series of concentric circles. Previous donors to the institution are in that innermost circle, then donors who are affiliated with it (through some "Friends of" organization), then individuals who already are receiving services from this institution, then potential donors believed to be interested in institutions like this. In all cases, special attention is given to targets who are close to members of the board or the administration.

Usually the fundraiser will show the potential donor the pyramid and ask, "Where do you see yourself on this?" That makes it, often, a self-solicitation process. But that self-appraisal can shift. We know of one lavish campaign for a museum in New York, and the chair of the museum started out pledging $5 million and ended up giving over $20 million, much to his own mystification. But leaders need to lead. Donors can send a message with their gifts that is more potent than the money.

Knowing that, solicitors can get greedy. Many times, Charles has been asked for gifts that are larger than ones he wants to give. In one case, he was asked to contribute to a major capital campaign for a university. He decided that $5 million would be the right amount, but the fundraiser told Charles that such a gift from him would "destroy the campaign" by lowering the standard for everyone else. "Then I'll make life easier for you by withdrawing my gift entirely," Charles told him.

Suddenly the fundraiser became much more amenable.

Fundraisers also have to be careful not to ask for too little. Jeff made that mistake thirty years ago when he asked a wealthy individual for $100,000. Although that was the equivalent of three times that today, the man said yes so quickly that Jeff knew he should have asked for much more.

Like the gifts to the President's Fund, some restricted gifts can seem unrestricted, which invariably makes the recipient all the happier. If you want to endow a chair at Columbia University, Columbia would be thrilled because your gift has now freed up the money that would otherwise go to support that professor, money the administration can now use however it likes.

And the principle works more broadly. If you want to give some money to the cardiac rehabilitation clinic that provided end-stage care to your mother, the hospital could, in its accounting, ascribe a portion of the gift to overhead, freeing that portion for other uses.

Such restricted gifts can lead to some tough calls on the part of the receiving institution, for some of the restrictions are so tight as to compromise what the institution may see as its own goals and purposes. Some years ago, a foundation offered a museum $42 million for a new Louvre-like entrance. Adding to the pressure, the foundation had secured a further commitment from the government to come through with an additional $8 million for the project. But there was a catch: the design did not fit the mission and vision of the museum as defined by the new director and his board. The board concurred and turned it down. The museum found that money, and more, elsewhere and has undertaken major construction that perfectly fits with the director's and board's goals. The lesson: Always follow your mission, never the money. Management, after all, is about doing things right; leadership is about doing the right things.

To avoid such catastrophes, any donor has to begin to discuss her plans with the intended recipient well before the gift is made, so it doesn't become extortion in reverse (essentially, "I've given you this money. Now do what I say"). A nonprofit must follow the mission to fulfill its responsibility.

At the Philanthropies, we have found ourselves on the wrong side of this. A university came to us to ask for a $1 million gift to help enact the mission of its new president; we offered $2 million if the university could conduct a program that worked for it in the new framework and also advanced some strategic purposes of its own. The university officials said sure; they knew exactly the department to handle it. The university happily took the money, and we happily gave it. Then—disappointment. The department in question proved to be poorly equipped for the work, and uninterested besides. The project never got going, and we were not pleased. But that is the hazard of an organization chasing money: the university was so eager for the Philanthropies' money, it made promises that it could not meet. The university has since tried us again, but we have demurred. Fool me once . . .

The Endowment Gift

Other restricted gifts can have an appealing unrestricted quality. One of them is the endowment gift: money for endowment, meaning the corpus of the gift is to remain intact (unless other arrangements are specified), while the income may be used to fund general operations or some specific purpose that the donor designates. Endowment gifts also send a powerful signal that you as a donor believe in the institution and its future, so much so that you will provide support in perpetuity.

The open-ended nature of such an endorsement is why we're somewhat leery of such gifts. Who can say what will happen to the place when all the current leadership have died or moved on? Perpetuity is a long time.

The Restricted Endowment Gift

If you are determined that your endowment gift be reserved for a particular use, you can say so through a restricted endowment gift. This is a good way to make sure that a particular program that is meaningful to you—an initiative to encourage young people to take an interest in classical music, say—will be continued long after you and the current administration are gone.

Then again, times can change in unpredictable ways. Jeff used to administer a permanent endowment to support women with postpartum depression. Over time, however, fewer and fewer women suffered from the disorder because of increasingly effective medications and ever-better treatment at hospitals. Although postpartum depression largely ceased to be an issue, Jeff had to hire attorneys to persuade a judge to allow those funds to be broadened to other needs of new mothers.

If you insist on a restricted endowment gift, be sure to include an escape clause allowing your funds to be slid over to another program if yours no longer needs financial support.

Restricted capital gifts offer the same advantages and the same liabilities. One might imagine that a capital gift would be a monument that withstands the ages, but no. That spanking new

$30 million wing you so generously donated to the museum won't remain fresh forever, no matter how solid and timeless it may now seem. Eventually it will seem as dated as the wing it replaced—and it will itself be cleared away to make room for a yet more expensive, and probably even more solid, wing named for someone else, and your contribution will be reduced to a plaque on the wall where your wing once stood. From the institution's perspective, this is all to the good. It needs to be updated periodically. This may not be bad if you truly care about the institution. But if you care about your legacy, be sure the gift document spells out your precise expectation.

In any project, leaders are all important. And they are likely to be no less important to you if you are a major donor to the project. Keep that in mind when formulating any gifts. If you don't think a project could survive the departure of a certain leader, do your best to assure yourself he will see it through. Don't be shy about that.

The Event-Related Gift

Everyone has seen the invitations. They often come hand-addressed, with bold, eye-catching graphics, a few corporate sponsors, a lengthy benefit committee, its best-known members usually "honorary," a worthy cause, and a celebrity honoree. Recipients are asked to buy a table, a seat, or several seats, and to bring their friends.

This is the event-related gift.

Given the amount of money and time it takes to put on these extravaganzas, you might wonder if they are worthwhile. From the organization's perspective, they absolutely are, largely because they are time specific. The institution knows when the money will come in. Plus, it is an effective strategy for reaching out to new potential members and partisans. It is a friend raiser as much as it is a fundraiser.

These friends and funds do not come cheap, however. It can cost hundreds of dollars per person to put on the dinner, so the yield on a five hundred dollar ticket may be marginal. The organizers will likely need to have underwriters pick up most, if not all, of the costs of the dinner. Their core supporters will have to buy the expensive tables where the net proceeds are greatest, and in turn attract corporate supporters, who may have marketing budgets to support sponsorships. Ideally, the core supporters will sell tickets in bunches, with donors buying tables of ten.

For many organizations, the dinner is also a date certain by which annual campaign supporters must complete their gift, avoiding the painful slippage when no such date certain is in place.

CHAPTER 15

The Pudding Is in the Proof

Just as you can't drive a car without a speedometer, fuel gauge, and the other displays on the dashboard, you can't run a nonprofit without being able to tell when you're making progress and when you're not. "You can't improve what you can't measure," the late Michael Hammer, a wonderful organizational reengineering expert, used to say. Put another way, if you can't measure success, how will you know if you have achieved it?

We think of measurements of quality as a kind of graph paper that we place around an organization to determine whether it is advancing, retreating, or merely going sideways. But the graph paper we have in mind doesn't bear the standard grid coordinates. No, these are metrics specially chosen by the organization as its unique measure of progress. By deciding what it is that we seek to measure, we learn what it is we most strongly value. It's immensely helpful for a nonprofit to have those values in mind because they are the goals and objectives of the organization.

The Birthright Israel Program

It is not easy to decide on them, but it is essential that an organization go through the exercise, for the results end up defining everything it does. When we started the Birthright program, the one that annually sends tens of thousands of young adults of Jewish descent to Israel for an all-expenses paid ten-day trip, we did two things in this arena. First, we made program evaluation one of the five core elements of the program. Second, we carefully identified the goals, moved by the fact that, once proved, we were going to seek funding from others. At first, our partner, Michael Steinhardt, and our foundation covered all costs. Once we had demonstrated its efficacy, we wanted to bring in other donors, like the Government of Israel and various Jewish communities throughout the world. To attract them, we needed to clarify the mission and prove we could fulfill it. After much thought, we identified three essential goals for the program, each one of them measurable:

- After completing the trip, the participants feel a new or renewed connection to Israel.
- They experience an enhanced sense of their Jewish identity.
- They feel a closer connection to the Jewish people.

Taking the Measure of Success

Before the first airline ticket was purchased, we selected a first-rate research team at Brandeis University to perform the evaluation. Most such investigators are known to shape their results to conform to the hopes of their funders. But these—a two-person team—were known as the Dr. No's of the field, because they took such pleasure in strict methodology and integrity.

To us, the need to produce measurable and indisputable results was no burden; we welcomed the chance to prove ourselves to our donors. We believe strongly that donors have every right to know if a nonprofit is fulfilling their hopes with their gift. With a brand-new museum of design, for example, one donor may be a local developer looking to increase economic activity. That is understandable. Well, is there any? Another could be a patron of the arts eager for an uptick in design appreciation. Okay. Any proof of that? Still another might be the administration of a local university hoping to promote its own design program. Any sign of that? These are all legitimate objectives. Truth to tell, the donors themselves may not always be able to articulate their objectives so precisely, but it behooves the director of the museum, as it does executive directors of nonprofits everywhere, to think in terms of giving donors what they want, within the context of the organization's mission.

This is not crass. It is necessary, for it is all part of the intentionality that we encourage in donors to make their gifts purposefully. There is nothing shameful about having an agenda, as long as the agenda is consistent with the mission and vision of the organization. There is something shameful about not knowing what that agenda is.

So with Birthright, we knew from the beginning that measurement was essential. But how do you measure something like Jewish identity or connection to Israel? Was it like Justice Potter Stewart's definition of pornography: that you know it when you see it? In this case, the students knew it if they felt it. Well, how would anyone know that they felt it more than they would have anyway?

And here we were in luck. For unlike most other experiments in the social sciences, we were blessed with what experimenters call controls: individuals who are virtually identical to the subjects under scrutiny who can be used for comparison purposes. With Birthright, we had thirteen thousand applicants for the eight thousand slots in the first year, with the winners selected at random by lottery. So we had the perfect controls: the five thousand young adults who didn't go but were nearly identical to those who did. A point-to-point comparison would yield the difference that Birthright had made. Those comparisons were heartening.

How much has Birthright added to a feeling of connection to Israel? A lot, according to *Ten Days of Birthright Israel,* a book written on the Birthright phenomenon by esteemed educational consultant Barry Chazan and Len Saxe, director of the Maurice and Marilyn Cohen Center for Modern Jewish Studies at Brandeis University. The number of Birthrighters who said it had affected them "very much" or "to a great extent" in this regard was nearly twice that of the controls one year out. Different from what one might have expected, the ratio increased somewhat over time. The change relating to the connection to the Jewish people was less profound, but still significant.

The Product

For our own purposes, we also thought it important to evaluate the product itself, meaning the experience of the trip, aside from the lasting philosophical changes it delivered. We identified them as three: input, throughput, and output. We already had the selection criteria that accounted for the input: the kinds of students we started with. And here we were bent on luring the unlikely candidate—the student who never imagined that he would ever want to go on a ten-day trip to Israel. We left to others the true zealots. We wanted the casual participant. If we could convert her into a passionate believer in the cause of Israel, we would really accomplish something significant.

We closely monitored the throughput, the trips themselves, to make sure they reached the level of quality we were seeking. We had a team from McKinsey & Company, on a pro bono basis, help us set up appropriate measures. We did not run the trips ourselves, so we didn't have full real-time control over them. We were the franchiser, turning the trips themselves over to franchisees, whom we gave thick manuals spelling out our exacting requirements for a Birthright experience. The manual covered everything: education, guides, rooms, housing, security. By spelling everything out, we also established the standards for it. It became measurable. Charles knew well from his father that organizations do not stay flat. They improve or they deteriorate. He was determined that Birthright Israel was going to be a learning organization, striving for continuous improvement.

Our general philosophy is to be tight to be loose to be tight. We were tight in the sense that at the highest level, we had a clear vision for the program: someday to bring every Jewish young adult between ages eighteen and twenty-six to Israel for their first living-and-learning trip. We were loose in that we allowed a great deal of flexibility in the ways that the trip operators met our requirements. They could be nonprofit or for profit, religiously focused or culturally focused. We didn't care how our subcontractors accomplished our objectives; we cared only that they did. Thus, the structure became tight once more. This leeway led to a wide variety of styles and emphases. An individual trip organizer might operate trips that featured extreme sports or long bicycle trips. Another might focus on medical students or might draw participants from a particular American city.

Again, regardless of the style of the trip, we wanted it to be uniformly tightly run and of high quality. All hotels had to be three-star. And we measured everything from whether there were first-aid kits on the bus to the quality of the food. On many buses, we placed an observer on board to monitor things, and, of course, her very existence influenced the outcome as the operators tried to improve their performance knowing she was present.

Inevitably there were some problems. For the summer of 2008, an outpouring from generous donors allowed us to double the number of participants from fourteen thousand to over twenty-eight thousand. While this was heartening, it came when improved security in Israel made it an appealing destination again, forcing us to compete frantically for the best tour guides and hotels and imperiling the quality we prized. In the end, our measurements showed that we reached our goals for those trips that year, but at some cost to the organization.

To Define Success Is to Measure It

You may think of success as an abstraction, but it really isn't. It can always be defined in terms of the objectives you seek. If you're involved with a nonprofit, you always have some objective in mind, be it to expand the Little League in your area, or stop teenage smoking, or protect the habitat of the piping plover. But that objective is not worthy if you can't tell how you're doing as you go about achieving it. The objective should have a yardstick attached, much like the United Way thermometers that tell how well a fund drive is doing.

To us, there are three basic sets of measures.

The first is *accessibility*. By that, we don't mean something as straightforward as wheelchair ramps for the disabled. It's much more complex but no less essential. It's a combination of outreach and facilitation in order to draw in the highest possible percentage of the population you seek to serve. It's probably easiest to explain with an example.

When Jeff was running a geriatric community mental health center in Florida, his funders and he were worried that the program was underserving the Cuban members of the local catchment area. The center had done all the obvious things to attract them— making sure that all printed materials were available in Spanish and that the word about the center was getting out.

When the center investigated further, it discovered that Cubans resisted coming in for mental health treatment for cultural reasons. They didn't necessarily consider seeking this kind of treatment shameful, but it did have negative associations. In Cuba, such services are dispensed at a single state hospital that is so badly run and outmoded that even people who desperately need those services stay away. So the Cubans in Florida avoided the center too. Also, there was a tradition of *personalismo* that discouraged referrals to an impersonal-seeming institution like the mental health center. It was far better to refer a client to an individual practitioner whom the referrer knew personally.

Some Spanish-speaking social workers were dispatched into the Cuban service community. When they encountered anyone with mental health issues, they would direct that person not to the center but to a particular psychotherapist at the center. And he gave her that therapist's number and promised to call her in advance. That increased the count of Hispanic patients who could be helped, and the center became more successful. Similarly, keeping the clinic open late two evenings a week bumped up numbers even more, as its original 8:30 to 5:30 schedule had conflicted with many people's work schedules.

Beyond accessibility is *acceptability*. The services of a nonprofit need to be good. They need to be delivered on time, courteously, and professionally; communication needs to be clear; and they need to yield the hoped-for results. Jeff was constantly evaluating the center's basic services. Were people satisfied? Did they have to wait long to be seen? Were they pleased with their care? Did

181

doctors explain things to them well? Did they feel heard? All of this information was captured and used to make poor performance better and good performance better still.

The third element is *outcomes.* Results. Performance. Nothing else matters if you don't deliver the goods. Once you have established your objectives, you need to set up measures to determine if you have attained them. These yardsticks are essential to determining what's productive and what's not. Unfortunately, the results aren't always easy to assess. Results of an experiment in the physical sciences may be precise; they are less so in humanistic areas like education, culture, and the social sciences where much philanthropy takes place. But their difficulty doesn't make them any less important.

As an example, together with the Righteous Persons Foundation, we began a program called Reboot that was meant to take creative Jewish people from a variety of fields—literature, journalism, social networking, music, television—who were, all of them, on the cutting edge of their fields, and expose or reexpose them to their Judaism in the hope that their renewed connection would inspire them to use their creativity to "reboot" Jewish life among the young.

Did it work? That assessment got very messy. We first wanted to know whether our participants were indeed getting turned on to their Judaism and whether this was affecting how they saw themselves. Even that was hard to say. We'd hoped that a simple questionnaire would suffice to determine the answer. The outside evaluation firm had to interview the participants in person and also get them to respond to an elaborate e-mail survey in order to capture more of the nuances of their responses. They concluded that first year that 87 percent were "profoundly impacted" by the Reboot experience. As to the more important question—whether the participants' behaviors had shifted any because of Reboot—there was very little movement there, much to our disappointment.

As we thought further, we realized the truth of the matter: that slight as it was, the behavioral change conformed to a standard U-shaped curve, a favorite of social scientists. This reflects the basic sociological fact that significant change occurs only to a few; most show only modest change, and some show none at all.

At the extremes, however, the effect was powerful, and we took heart from it. One woman decided that all Jews should create an "ethical will" that charted their moral intentions. This year, she decided that during the Jewish high holidays between Rosh Hashanah and Yom Kippur, people should have the opportunity to keep a kind of moral log on a computer program that could be pulled off the Web. She called it 10Q, and each day it posed an ethical question like, "How can you make the world a little more beautiful?" You record your answer on the Web site, where it is stored until the next Rosh Hashanah. Then you can pull it back out to see what you have done to act on your aspirations.

Still, for us, a smattering of innovations like this wasn't enough. We wanted to see more than glimpses of success. We wanted those people, as thought leaders, to take their renewed commitment to Judaism out into the world and make a difference. We are nearly a decade into this now, and they are finally beginning to. We were thrilled that in 2008, the new Contemporary Jewish Museum in San Francisco asked to partner with Reboot to create an innovative launch; seven thousand young people arrived for a night of study and waited in lines out the door. The evaluations were outstanding and indicated that something was spreading from these thought leaders to others. Now that Reboot is well established, we have shifted from being active funders who set the direction of the organization to passive ones who simply provide funding. But we have continued to insist on regular and robust evaluation to make sure the program remains on track.

Information Is Power

At the mental health center, Jeff found that it wasn't always easy to accumulate the assessment data he believed were necessary to maintain high-quality service. The therapists often resented the intrusion, believing they alone should be able to determine the quality of the care they were providing. And the leadership was sympathetic to their position. The amount of paperwork that anyone in health care has to fill out is appalling. But we nevertheless believe that the data on quality are essential; otherwise, leadership is flying blind. Burdensome as it may be to have staffers use their time on questionnaires, it would be even more burdensome if they didn't. The organization would likely lose a lot of time, money, and energy trying to find its way—and that would be far more to the detriment of staffers than the bother of filling out forms. Furthermore, self-reflection is a valued characteristic, and evaluation motivates those providing services to reflect on their performance.

Increasingly people are coming to recognize this. We have funded a personalized medicine initiative at Mount Sinai Medical Center, run by a skillful investigator named Erwin Bottinger. First, we asked him to establish annual objectives and then make the necessary assessment to determine if he had met them. We were afraid that Dr. Bottinger might balk at such an encumbrance, but he had no objection, believing that such data could help him too. The best such investigators welcome the partnership with donors that help them become better at what they do. Too often the nonprofit feels threatened by an evaluation, for fear that it will lose its funding if it ever comes up short. But we aren't draconian about it. We believe that you can learn from your mistakes. Start-ups, for example, rarely get it right the first time, which is why Silicon

Valley has the motto, "Fail often to succeed sooner." But with the suppleness necessary to adjust to any disappointing results, those nonprofits can find their way to success.

Birthright has been tremendously successful, but we doubt it would have done nearly so well if it hadn't come on the heels of a similar program we tried called The Israel Experience, which was a disaster. One reason it failed was that its objectives were not intricately tied to its essential elements—its operations, partners, and economic model. Funding partners failed to meet their obligations, trip organizers decided everything for themselves, and the high school kids who were the participants turned to their parents for guidance since they were not used to being off on their own, thereby creating a second market that we couldn't reach. It quickly became chaos—and all too clear that despite an infusion of funds, we had a failure on our hands, in that the number of participants did not grow. But we learned from our mistakes, and when we tried again with Birthright, we got it right, largely by doing it differently the second time around. We determined the approach before bringing on funding partners, imposed strict controls on trip organizers, and selected older, more independent students who wouldn't rely on their parents.

While we have spoken of the importance of evaluation for non-profits, it is no less important for donors, who also are concerned that their money is being spent wisely. Again, the nonprofit realm lacks the bottom-line measures of for-profits, but that doesn't mean it lacks any measures at all. The measures it has can be immensely useful in helping the donor determine the value of her gift. If, for example, you have given ten thousand dollars to a community outreach program, the organization should be able to tell you how many people were served because of it. That's harder to assess if you give to a larger institution like, say, the San

Francisco Museum of Modern Art, where your money can get lost amid all the commingled funds. But even there, you can probably find a smaller department or program within the museum where your gift would make a measurable difference—in children's art programs, for instance, or European prints from the nineteenth century. There, the museum can tell you exactly what it has done with the money and what difference it has made. Indeed, one of the reasons that the United Ways and United Jewish Appeals of the world are falling behind is that they usually can't tell you what they have done with *your* money. And that can be frustrating to donors, who can be left with the impression that their gift didn't really matter. But as the new philanthropy ascends, nonprofits are coming to realize that quantified results are important to donors, and they are doing better at providing them.

Ironically, good evaluation can attract donors. In the Birthright program, three donors who had declined to participate after the first year, our dry run, later came in with multimillion-dollar gifts after they had the chance to review the evaluation results. They were Wall Street professionals and serious numbers guys who weren't going to get involved until they saw the quantitative results (even though past results are no guarantee of future returns!).

Sad to say, one reason that such measurements are essential is that there is so little trust anymore. There are any number of explanations, from Watergate to the culture of greed. But we attribute some of the pervasive distrust to the fact that students aren't taught civics anymore. That lack of a civic knowledge—the awareness of how society is legally bound together by the U.S. Constitution—has led to a lack of civic engagement. People are disconnected from a larger community beyond their immediate neighbors, friends, and family, one in which philanthropy naturally plays an essential part. Instead, we are only with the individual, and a rather distrustful one at that, and at every turn, she needs to be convinced she is not being taken for a ride. (It didn't help philanthropy that Bill Aramony, the past head of the United Way, was convicted of fraud and embezzlement not long after the rising Gen Xers came to awareness.)

But it is on facts that trust can be built back up with hard numbers that produce the solid evidence of positive change. Such measurements provide the foundation for a new faith in philanthropy and, perhaps through that, the beginnings of a restoration of trust in civic life more broadly.

CHAPTER 16

A Little Financial Advice

IF YOU'RE LIKE MOST OTHER DONORS, you don't mind taking advantage of the many tax benefits of your philanthropy. And why not? The U.S. government recognizes that private charity benefits everyone, and it has fashioned the tax laws to reflect that fact.

The advice that follows can get technical in spots, and you may not need to take in all of it. So again, feel free to skip ahead to the aspects of the tax laws—in giving land, say, or appreciated securities—that are of particular interest to you. Please remember, however, that neither of us is a tax lawyer, and that any financial move you are considering should be run by someone who is. Furthermore, we are offering only general and hypothetical examples that may not be pertinent to potential donors in every state and every income level.

For donors who are considering making substantial gifts, certain limitations to the deductions that may be allowed should be taken into account. These limitations range from 20 percent to 50 percent of the donor's adjusted gross income, depending on the type of

While this chapter is designed for U.S. readers, Canadian readers are invited to
www.artofgivingbook.com for a supplement, which adapts these points to a Canadian framework.

charity to which the gift is made, the nature of the property being contributed, and the use of the property by the charity. For example, the deduction for a cash gift to a donor-advised fund is limited to 50 percent of the donor's adjusted gross income, while the deduction for an identical cash gift to a private foundation would be limited to 30 percent of the donor's adjusted gross income. Contributions in excess of the allowable limitations may be carried over for the next five years.

Writing a Check

By far the simplest deduction is the one that comes from writing a check to a nonprofit (after making sure that it has been accorded that tax status as an official 501(c)3, of course). Keep the check for your records, and then, at tax time, deduct the sum from your gross income. That reduces your taxes by a portion determined by your tax rate. If you donate $100 and deduct that full amount and you're in a 28 percent tax bracket, you have shaved $28 off your federal tax obligation. For contributions above $250, you must have verification of the gift from the charity, along with a statement indicating that you have received no benefits related to the gift. (So if you give to go to one of the benefit dinners, don't expect Uncle Sam to pay for his share of the dinner costs. That is subtracted from the cost of the ticket to yield the true charitable value of the gift, which is the portion that is deductible.)

If you are mailing that check, make sure the postmark is before January 1 and is from the U.S. Postal Service. If you use a nongovernmental courier service such as FedEx, the donation counts when the charity receives the check, not when FedEx picks it up. Postdating a check does not help. For those making cash contributions at year end, a credit card may be a safe, verifiable, and convenient option.

Appreciated Securities

Maybe instead of cash, you want to give stock, stock with a significant gain—an "appreciated security," like a share of MMR (Make Me Rich, Inc.), say, that has increased in value. If you bought that share at $10 and it is now selling at $100, you have a built-in gain of $90 per share. If you'd simply sold that share and kept the proceeds, you'd have to pay capital gains tax on the $90. But if you give the share to your alma mater, then the college can sell the share and credit you for the full value of the share—and spare you the pain of paying the $13.50 or so in capital gains tax that you'd owe if you sold the share yourself. Thus, you get to deduct from your taxable income $100, resulting in a federal tax savings of $28, assuming the same tax bracket as in the example above. Appreciated assets therefore offer a "three-fer": you get credit for their full value, you get to deduct that full value, and you avoid paying any capital gain.

Retirement Plan Assets

In the words of Benjamin Franklin, "nothing can be said to be certain, except death and taxes." However, if you name a qualified charity as beneficiary of your IRA, 401-K, or certain other retirement accounts, your death may actually serve to diminish taxes. Most retirement accounts contain deferred income tax liabilities that are payable as the funds are distributed. On the death of the account owner, a retirement account left to one or more individuals may be subject to both income and estate tax liabilities, greatly diminishing the value of the assets distributable to the beneficiaries. When charities are named as beneficiaries of such accounts, the funds pass free of both income and estate tax to a worthy cause.

191

Donor-Advised Funds

You don't even need to give directly to your favorite charity. Instead, you can take advantage of the various donor-advised funds that serve as substitute foundations, holding your donations until you recommend where to direct them. Community foundations throughout the nation offer these services to donors and charities. Fidelity, Schwab, and many other investment fund houses now offer them through related tax-exempt public charities. You park your money in one of these donor-advised funds, and in that tax year, you take the tax deduction for the full value of the gift. Later, when you have decided on the causes to which you would like to deliver the funds, you "recommend" where to send the money. The fund has the responsibility to be sure that your recommendation is going to a legitimate tax-exempt entity and that you are not getting anything in return.

We use the word *recommend* because, strictly speaking, these funds are no longer yours. They belong to the community foundation or fund to which you've "given" them. Consequently, you can't tell the fund to send a thousand dollars to the Red Cross; you can only "advise" it to do that—hence the name. The advice is invariably followed, but the locution reveals the essential truth of the arrangement. We have two cautions on this type of gift. First, there is no second deduction for this gift when it is ultimately made to a charity; your ticket gets punched only once. And, second, once you have put the money in a donor-advised fund, you can't take it back out for your personal use. Such limitations aside, these funds act so much like personal foundations that many donors use them that way, sparing themselves the expense and hassle of setting up their own foundation.

It is in this realm of appreciated assets that matters can get quite complex for the donor, so complex that if the gift you have in mind gets anywhere close to six figures, you should probably gather a team of professionals to advise you, even beyond the tax lawyer we recommended above. A financial planner would certainly be advisable, but also an estate lawyer (even for people under forty years old who would otherwise not be thinking of estate planning), and an accountant.

Gifts of Physical Assets

There is a wide range of assets that appreciate in value and which donors have passed along to the charities of their choice in place of cash. In some cases, the organization doesn't sell the object but keeps it just as it is. An art museum might be very happy to have some Robert Motherwells to add to its collection or an archive overjoyed to receive some papers of John Adams. In giving them, as with the appreciated stock, the donor can deduct the full selling price. Even if the Motherwells were purchased for just a few hundred dollars when the artist was still obscure, the donor can claim the full valuation of however many millions his work now commands. An important caveat: in the case of art, this is true only if the donor gives the work to an art institution, and one that will actually display it. After a series of abuses, the IRS has become quite strict about this. If the art does not go to an art museum on that basis, the donor can deduct only the original selling price, which is likely to be far less.

We should also note that in any one tax year, the donor can take the deduction only up to a dollar value equaling *half* his adjusted gross income, although he can carry forward that deduction on that basis for five years.

As for determining that valuation, just as different realtors will give you different estimates for the price of your house, so do different appraisers. In the case of the painting, for example, a museum that had a particular interest in completing a Motherwell collection with your painting would value it more highly than a museum that specialized in nineteenth century landscapes and had little interest in Motherwells—and probably more highly than an independent auction house like Christie's or Sotheby's. The rule of thumb is that the appraiser must be independent from the donor and the charity and the financial worth of the object must be the fair market value as of the date of the gift.

One Art Connoisseur's Tale

In 1973, Donald Jonas helped develop Lechter's, a national chain of household goods stores that flourished for a quarter-century until it succumbed to competitive pressures from larger chains, like Bed, Bath & Beyond, Target, and Walmart. By then, Donald and his wife, Barbara, had moved to a larger apartment and developed an interest in art. Uninformed when they started, they educated themselves by taking courses, reading books, and going to museums and galleries where they started to buy. Before long, the Jonases had accumulated quite a collection of de Koonings, Klines, Rothkos, and work by other prominent abstract expressionists. The years were passing, and the Jonases didn't want to leave the paintings—which Donald called his "friends"—in their estate for their lawyers to distribute after their death. At the same time, Donald was developing an interest in philanthropy, with a particular focus on nursing, so he decided to sell off some of the paintings to raise funds for his charitable efforts.

Here's where the tax laws come in. If the Jonases' paintings were to go to a museum or an art school or any other institution that is art related, they could get a full deduction for the fair market value of the art; however, the art would be held by the institution. But if he were to give them to some other organization like the Jewish Communal Fund, a community foundation he liked, he could deduct only the original price he paid for them, often many years back when the artists were obscure and the prices low. The Jonases wanted to sell the paintings to raise as much cash as possible for his charity work, but if they sold the paintings through an auction house, they would not have received any deduction at all.

The solution? He decided to give fifteen of the paintings to the Jewish Communal Fund after all. It sold the paintings at Christie's for a stunning $44 million. As a charity, the fund skipped any sales tax and kept all the proceeds. Since it was a donor-advised fund, the Jonases could recommend how the money should be invested and spent. The Jonases decided it was sufficient just to take the deduction on the original purchase price. As Laura Paulson, international director for Christie's, put it: "This extraordinary collection, which has given these collectors a lifetime of pleasure and beauty, will continue to give in a new dimension . . . to improve the lives and the well being of many."

Donating Land

The land trust is a wonderful asset for the landscape, preserving open space forever. It is the product of thoughtful donors who are eager to keep their property pristine and safe from ever being developed—and happy to enjoy a substantial tax write-off too. The process is best explained by example. Let's say an elderly couple owns a hundred-acre spread in the Lehigh Valley in eastern Pennsylvania. They're getting on in years, their kids have moved away, but they want to keep their property out of the hands of developers after they die. So they deed eighty acres to a land trust to keep the property undeveloped, while they themselves get a substantial deduction for the appreciated value of the gift. Still, as with the gift of a painting, any deduction from the sale of land is limited to half their adjusted gross income that tax year—and for each of the next four years afterward.

Remarkably, you can give it away—and still keep it. Donors can gift their land to a charitable institution like a local college if it will lease the property back to the donors until they die. The owners receive a deduction for the increased value of the land they have purchased, subject to the restriction of half-income for five years, and they remain in their home.

A similarly paradoxical arrangement can be worked out for art. Rather than give your cherished Mondrian to the Museum of Modern Art, you can gift a partial interest on the condition that you can retain a proportional literal possession annually for up to ten years. So even after you give it away, it stays exactly where it has always been, on your wall over the couch in your living room. You can deduct the proportionate share of the fair market value, subject to the previous income restrictions. Although the remaining portion of the gift is consummated at a future time, your deduction is against your income tax now rather than your estate later. Since the museum has a "partial interest" in the gift, it could conceivably ask for the "entire interest," which is legal-speak for coming into your home and taking their painting off your wall for that portion of the year which it owns. But that may be unlikely if the director expects any other donors to gift their paintings on a similar basis.

144 Shares

While giving stock is fairly straightforward, there are some extra possibilities for the preferred stock known as "144 shares" because of the Securities and Exchange Commission regulation that governs them. These are restricted shares that are generally owned by the principals of a firm—the founders, key employees, initial shareholders—and are restricted in the sense that they cannot be readily sold on the open market. The owners can, however, donate them to a charity and receive a tax deduction that tax year. The charity is then obligated to hold on to these restricted shares for a certain period of time, usually a year, and then it can sell the shares on the open market for cash.

Giving Jewelry

While securities, art, and land are three of the most popular assets to donate to a nonprofit, there are many others. Indeed, almost anything of value can be given to the charity of your choice. Jewelry is one. That requires only an appraisal by a reputable dealer. With it, you can give your great aunt's diamond brooch to the Natural History Museum in Philadelphia and get a deduction for the full appraised value. If the museum chooses not to display the piece, it may then sell it to a dealer and use the proceeds to expand its endowment or fund programs. Because the IRS has grown to be suspicious of such transactions, it is best, even in the case of a prestigious recipient like the Natural History Museum, to turn to a reputable, independent appraiser to determine the market value.

The Lusty Connoisseur

Years ago we knew one self-styled patron of the arts, who was actually a patron of the arts of one artist in particular, a rather comely young Spanish painter. Every year, he bought ten of her paintings. Of the ten, he'd keep eight and give one each to two of his best friends. They, in turn, put their paintings up for auction at a prominent auction house. The three then would sit in the audience, and when the Spaniard's pictures came up for sale, they would bid against each other, wildly pushing up the price to extraordinary levels. In paying so much for the two paintings, the threesome had established a high price for all of the Spaniard's work, including the remaining eight paintings our patron possessed. He could then take a hefty deduction when he gave them away to various museums, which were grateful to receive art of such stunning value. The deduction substantially cut his tax obligations and freed up enough cash so he could lavish attention on the lovely painter.

This loophole, along with others, was closed over the years. However, it reminds us that the artificial inflation of the present-day value of a gift and other abuses of charitable giving cheats everyone: the citizens by skimping on the taxes that should have been paid, the legitimate charities that are undermined every time this occurs, and everyone who is gypped out of an expression of genuine acts of generosity and not repelled by fraudulent ones.

Donating Your Car

You've probably heard the pitch: instead of selling your used-up old car, give it to the local public radio station, inner-city health clinic, or arts organization. Unless the charity uses the car for another purpose like delivering food to seniors or donating the car to help an individual keep a job, generally your deduction is limited to the proceeds from the sale. You get the deduction, and the nonprofit gets the value of the car. So goes the pitch. The only problem is that the nonprofit doesn't get the full value of the car. Not being in the business of buying or selling cars, the nonprofit assigns that task to a middleman, who may take as much as 90 percent of the proceeds, giving the remainder to the nonprofit. Beware.

Intellectual Property

There are plenty of intangibles to take to the nonprofit marketplace as well, such as intellectual property. The songs of Richard Rogers, for example, went to sustain a Richard Rogers Foundation. Book rights, copyright, patents—all of these can provide considerable income over time for a charity.

Choosing the Right Foundation for You

For the lucky few who are considering starting their own private foundation to dispense their gifts, they should know that it doesn't make much sense unless you have at least $1 million a year to give away or the foundation you are contemplating is part of your multimillion estate plan. Anything less, and the legal fees and overhead keep it from making sense. But if you do have that much to put into philanthropy, you will need to decide if you would rather create a private grant-making foundation, or a private operating foundation.

What is the difference?

The grant-making foundation is just that: it makes grants in areas of its interest and is obliged by IRS rules to disburse a minimum of 5 percent of its assets annually on program and administration. Most foundations spend no more, a fact that should give government policymakers pause. Five percent really isn't much, especially if you consider that the government is forgoing the taxes on the appreciated assets that went into the foundation. It should go without saying that when it comes to philanthropy, society should benefit, not lose.

The operating foundation, by contrast, may make few, if any, grants. It devotes its resources to providing charitable services directly. When funding operating foundations, the IRS allows donors to deduct up to 50 percent of their adjusted gross income.

Charitable Trusts

There are some charitable trusts that we do not even mention because they are so complex. Indeed, because of their complexity, they are now being superseded by donor-advised funds, which are much simpler and cheaper to operate. Donors are still turning to a variety of charitable trusts to fulfill their giving objectives. Like donor-advised funds, they operate as mini-foundations. Unlike donor-advised funds, the money is still yours. You are free to decide for yourself whether you would like to hold on to the principal for your children and distribute only the income to charity, or pass the income to your children and reserve the principal for charity.

There are three major vehicles:

—♋—

- *Charitable lead trusts.* Here the charity is first in line, receiving the income generated by a particular sum of assets, while the principal will be delivered to a noncharitable beneficiary, like the donor's children or a cherished friend, when the donor dies. Depending on the manner in which the CLT is structured, it may provide the donor with a current income tax deduction and/or transfer tax benefits.
- *Charitable remainder trusts.* Now the arrangement runs the other way: the noncharitable beneficiary (like the children again) is first in line to receive the income, and the charity is ultimately bequeathed the remaining principal, at the donor's death. A CRT may provide an immediate income tax deduction for present value of the remainder interest passing to charity. Also, because a CRT is exempt from tax on its investment income, appreciated securities held by a CRT may be sold without incurring capital gains taxes, often allowing for a significantly increased income yield. Some donors use the increased income to purchase life insurance, enabling them to both provide for their family and make a sizable charitable gift.
- *Pooled income fund.* This works like a tax-free municipal bond, except the bond in this case is generally offered by a more established and more sophisticated nonprofit institution, often a university or a museum. In exchange for a substantial donation, the nonprofit institution will return a fixed percentage in interest for the donor's lifetime. On the death of the donor, the funds remain with the charity.

For Further Advice . . .

If you're puzzled, as you may well be, a range of philanthropic advisors specialize in navigating these uncertain waters for donors. Be wary, though, for they themselves aren't always especially reliable. Like certain unscrupulous investment advisors, some steer their clients into a nonprofit entity not because it is objectively better for the donor but because they have a stake in it, making it better for them. Lawyers, for example, are sometimes inclined to steer you toward more complicated trusts, since that can create high-paid work for them. A more sensible way may be to go through your local community foundation, which tends to be markedly more dispassionate and serves a variety of nonprofits in the community, at relatively low cost. Independent philanthropic advisors are also a good resource. One group of financial advisors we like is the Rockefeller Philanthropy Advisors, which grew out of the Rockefeller-related foundations and family office to take on outside clients, and now has a staff of sixty and offices all over the country. They'll advise you on your giving and even set up a "back office" to run that giving for you.

To evaluate others, given the wide range of talents and reliability, you probably need to do what you would do to check out any professional who is unknown to you: Google the person, consult references, and ask friends who have used her. You'd be wise to go through the list of charities she has recommended to clients. If you see the same charity listed on different accounts, it may be because she has an interest in that organization. Indeed, for this advisor, "conflict of interest" means where there's no conflict, there's no interest!

CHAPTER 17

On Innovations

THE BUSINESS OF PHILANTHROPY IS BUSINESS. That notion is often lost when you see those ubiquitous ads showing the swollen belly of a hungry child or a child with a hideously misshapen smile. Images like that can go straight to your heart. But in so doing, they often bypass your brain. You can't just hand the first child some money to go get something to eat, or send the second to an oral surgeon to fix his smile. You have to think through the delivery system, establish whether it is likely to be adequately funded, determine its capability, and decide if it is sufficiently effective to address problems like those. And this is even aside from the larger question, of whether these issues are the ones that really move you.

No less than for-profit businesses in their endless quest for competitive advantage, the many elements of nonprofits that go into its delivery system are constantly challenged to keep up with the fresh demands for rigor in the new philanthropy. And it is impressive to consider the wide array of assistance presently available on a variety of issues (see Resource A for a full list). Among them, consider the following areas:

- *Technical.* For all the modern machinery from routers to GPS, there are organizations like Ashoka that help and train social entrepreneurs.

- *Giving.* Donors' circles operate like investment clubs, bringing some camaraderie to the hard business of choosing which charities to back.
- *Human capital.* New organizations like our own Slingshot, which select those few next-generation young adults going on their families' foundation boards, create a peer group for them and teach the basics of strategic philanthropy.
- *Funding efficiencies.* Infrastructure organizations are in existence only to make the philanthropic sector function more efficiently and effectively.
- *Philanthropic mentoring.* A range of new consultants, including Rockefeller Philanthropy Advisors, has risen up.
- *Revenue building.* This is philanthropy for profit, an oxymoron brought to us by Silicon Valley entrepreneurs, among others. One example is for-profit microloans to women in developing countries.
- *Program-related investments.* These have been incubated by the Ford Foundation and others as another way to achieve positive outcomes through the investment side of the foundation activity. We've been doing one of our own: it put up $1 million as collateral for small business loans to Israeli Arabs and women who wanted to start their own business. The loan repayment is a phenomenal 97 percent. We invested our $1 million in 6 percent bonds, and it gave banks the confidence to loan the qualified applicants $12 million. That's a twelve-to-one leverage for funds that will be returned to us. Our forgone return on this investment covers the administration costs. Not bad.
- *Scale.* This option is available to only a few. The new scale of modern philanthropy means that organizations like the Gates Foundation have more influence in the areas they serve

than does the U.S. government. When Bill Gates lands in the Ethiopian capital of Addis Ababa, the president greets him at the airport.

Clear as Glass

Aside from these individual developments, there is one overarching new idea: a belief in the value of clarity. In this, philanthropy has taken on some of the better characteristics of business. At ACBP, we keep good, clear records and try to measure outcomes so our success can be appraised. But clarity means an organizational clarity, specifying the roles of participants and thus defining their expectations. Instead of just loosely referring to every contributor as a "partner" regardless of role, we are finally beginning to distinguish between a general partner, who has a management function, and a limited partner, who is limited to a financial contribution— and getting back whatever psychic returns he can muster.

There is financial transparency too—one that is coming to the entire nonprofit sector, whether it welcomes it or not. Through the GuideStar Web site, you can now delve into the tax return of every nonprofit in the land (with the exception of those of a religious nature), seeing the total expenses, the balance sheet, the compensation of the five most senior officials. Everything that is on the tax return is there. While this has been enabled by the Internet revolution, it has been instigated by larger foundations like the Ford, Packard, Kellogg, and other foundations that have been determined to shed more light on the internal workings of nonprofits. This impulse is now spreading around the world. With the IRS's new, expanded 990 form for nonprofits, even more information will be available to the public.

Such clarity is a spur to ever-greater efficiency and effectiveness, squeezing all the more out of every dollar, since these results are now more widely apparent. Grantmakers for Effective Organizations and the Center for Effective Philanthropy (CEP) are two organizations that have been strong promoters of the idea that nonprofits should make the most of their resources. CEP was started by Mark Kramer, an investment advisor, and Michael Porter, the renowned Harvard Business School professor who specializes in business strategy.

Both organizations promote measurements of grant-maker satisfaction, a development we highly favor. Ask the grantees how we are doing as a grant-making foundation, and they would say spectacularly, fearing that any other answer would endanger their grants. But CEP relies on detailed questionnaires and follow-up interviews that are done on a totally anonymous basis to formulate its evaluations. It then posts the results on its Web site along with comparable data from other foundations to produce a kind of Zagat guide to foundations. A cooperating foundation can see, practically at a glance, how it stacks up to comparable foundations. GrantCraft, a project of the Ford Foundation, has assembled more hands-on wisdom for grant making. The more that nonprofit activities can be benchmarked, the greater the efficiency that will emerge in the field.

Innovation City

To the extent that philanthropy now acts more like a business, it has Silicon Valley to thank for accelerating this trend. It was there in the 1990s that a number of budding philanthropists were emerging from successful careers with a lot of money, some free time, and a determination to bring some of their corporate wisdom to their philanthropic efforts. That approach has spread through much of the field, and it has been transformative.

Their initiative has led to the creation or expansion of nearly twenty-five organizations whose primary interest is to make foundations better by teaching them business practices ranging from using their investment strategy for social good to becoming more effective advocates for change. A national, Washington, D.C.-based organization called BoardSource (originally the National Center for Non-Profit Boards) rose up to provide a range of services, including offering guidelines and instruction to boards, recognizing that they are the dashboard controls and guidance systems of nonprofits.

Many local communities are doing something similar. A community foundation in San Diego has created a governance institute where all board members of the city's nonprofits can come for training or to hone their skills. Some San Diego funders are starting to require this as a condition of their donations.

As on the for-profit side, competition for what amounts to market share has been a spur to innovation. Operation Smile and Smile Train both do cleft palate surgery in the developing world, each one challenging the other to provide more effective treatments for more patients. Without competition, organizations grow complacent, assuming their way is the best way. With it, organizations seek efficiency, avoid waste, and search for innovation in the quest for competitive advantage. More is better.

Indeed, common wisdom is that there is too much duplication in the nonprofit sector, and nonprofits should be "forced" to merge. We find this both amusing and sad, as research shows that 60 to 80 percent of for-profit mergers fail. The unique culture of each organization and the power of the marketplace can both determine those that succeed and those that don't. Nonprofit mergers have their place but not as a funder-driven generalization.

New technology is changing the face of philanthropy, as it is changing the face of everything else. Many philanthropies now are exclusively virtual, consisting of a Web site and nothing else. Changing the Present (www.changingthepresent.org), an idea pushed by eBay's Meg Whitman, is intended to transform ceremonial gift giving. Instead of giving a token gift to a friend or relative, give that gift as a contribution to a worthy nonprofit to some truly needy individual. The Web site is a comprehensive catalogue of nonprofit offerings—medical care, food, fun, disaster relief, and dozens of others—at giftlike price points starting at twenty-five dollars. Dubbed "The thought that counts," the gift is sent in the name of the friend or relative, who receives a card of grateful acknowledgment.

Nonprofits watched with envy in the 2008 presidential campaign as Barack Obama raised over $700 million for his candidacy, much of it on the Internet. To garner such a sum, a nonprofit recipient needs first to have raised awareness in ways that only press-saturated celebrity presidential candidates can do. However, there are ways to make the system a tad more favorably inclined. Various e-marketing firms are teaching nonprofits how to tell their stories in pursuit of a savvy Web-based support network. The idea is to push the nonprofit into consciousness on the Web so that the search algorithms work in its favor.

Any number of social entrepreneurs have taken advantage of the Internet to create virtual organizations that consist of little more than a brilliant idea and an engaging Web site. DonorsChoose.org is one we especially like. It was created by Charles Best, a Bronx schoolteacher who was frustrated that there was so little money available for class projects, trips, and other sorts of extras that the best education entails. Like Meg Whitman with Changing the Present, he created a kind of virtual supermarket that would post the most promising proposals for such all-important extras in hopes of attracting what he terms "citizen philanthropists" to contribute to them. The needs are modest: $417 for twenty-five copies of the novel *Holes* for an elementary school class in Indiana; $168 for five Hot Dot pens and six Hot Dot activities for a phonics class in Maryland. According to the DonorsChoose.org Web site, over $28 million has been raised since its inception in spring 2000. By such means, a few hundred million dollars are now raised on many sites this way every year.

Much of it is to brand-new sites, but a good deal of it is traditional giving that has shifted over to the Web because it is easier. Now, if we want to give to the Red Cross after Hurricane Katrina, we do it online. We know from unhappy experience that people often imagine that it goes the other way too: that they can get money from a nonprofit for their personal needs if they apply online. Our office gets e-mails from people all the time, even though it says quite clearly on our Web site that we don't give to individuals. Despite such hassles, we expect that online donations will continue to increase dramatically.

Strength in Numbers

Just as technology can increase the reach and power of nonprofits, so can a variety of agencies boost the impact of the social entrepreneurs who create them. Ashoka is one of the most prominent ones. It believes that, as it says on its Web site, "Everyone is a Changemaker." To that end, since 1981, Ashoka has created fellowships to fund, educate, and support two thousand social entrepreneurs, and then linked them up in broad networks and provided infrastructural support to extend their influence. Founded in 1980 by Bill Drayton, a former Environmental Protection Agency administrator and McKinsey partner, it has risen from $50,000 a year to well over $30 million a year today and has as its major partners McKinsey, the prominent public relations firm Hill & Knowlton, and the global law firm Latham and Watkins.

Although Drayton coined the term *social entrepreneur,* Ashoka is by no means the only organization in the business of supporting social entrepreneurs. Echoing Green follows a similar formula, funding the work of 450 social entrepreneurs in their start-up phase. Like Ashoka, Echoing Green supports individuals, not organizations. Both organizations grew out of the Peace Corps and Vista programs of the Kennedy administration. The optimistic energy that Kennedy tapped for that initiative has now shifted to the nonprofit sector, which is much more conducive to the notion of empowering individuals. City Year and Teach for America capture this spirit for domestic initiatives in education.

Some of this same fervor shows up in the donor circles, which we have come to think of as the perfect symbol of the new philanthropy. Giving circles are elastic, shaped to whatever configuration the group decides. They complete their loop not just by joining forces in this endeavor but by giving back to society some of what they have drawn from it. There are over four hundred giving circles, and they are located everywhere from Moscow, Idaho, and Traverse City, Michigan, to Los Angeles and New York City. The ages start in the twenties and go up from there. And they run in size from the five-woman One Percent for Moms, in Brooklyn, New York, to the fifty-seven-member Latino Giving Circle hosted by the Chicago Community Trust in Chicago. The financial contributions vary widely, as well, from $150 a year to $100,000.

Although they are not numerous, the circles are a reflection of the new philanthropy in their innovation and flexibility. In pooling their knowledge along with their funds, the group is more than the sum of its parts. It offers a community that can counter some of the atomism of modern life. In so doing, it demonstrates an essential truth about the new philanthropy, which is that people want to get personally involved and do more than write checks.

A venture fund is a high-end version of a donor circle: it has a more specific set of objectives and more resources with which to accomplish them. Like a venture capitalist, a venture fund manager is much more risk tolerant than other financial backers of nonprofits, more likely to invest in a charity early, well before it has demonstrated results, and is generally okay with the prospect of losing money. To her, high risk is the best route to high reward. Only a venture fund can achieve the dramatic impact she is hoping for. Like a venture capitalist, she will spread the risk over a number of investments in hopes that one home run or two will compensate for all the strikeouts. The creators of a venture fund are likely to want to watch the basket each egg is in, taking a seat on the board from which to monitor their investment close up. Traditional funders may believe in our NIFO rule of noses in, fingers out. Not so the venture fund manager: she's got her nose in and her fingers in too.

Profitable Nonprofits

Revenue sources, always important, have become increasingly diversified. In recent years, nonprofits have relied on for-profit subsidiaries to produce revenue from within. The classic example is the museum shop, which has become key to museums' viability—and in cases like the Metropolitan Museum shops, have become a chain of stand-alone retail stores across the country. This becomes problematic when the Metropolitan's shop, which pays no taxes, is competing with a similar store that does. The benefit for the nonprofit is clear, but the benefit for society isn't always. Why should the YMCA have a tax advantage for a gym around the corner from Crunch, which pays the full tax freight?

Years back, when Jeff was director of a rehabilitation agency, the agency had six "businesses" that were designed to provide employment training for mentally ill clients. One of these had an exclusive contract to manufacture underwear for the U.S. Army. Under the terms of the contract, 90 percent of the workforce were psychiatric clients. But in the factory, those workers produced only a portion of the goods. The remaining 10 percent of the workforce delivered the remainder. Was it fair to award such a priority contract to a "factory" that relies on some healthy workers, just as a competitor might? Public policy is a system of carrots and sticks, and it needs to reflect the society we wish to see.

—◌—

Many of these innovations may seem obvious: to make use of for-profit techniques, exploit the Internet, encourage competition. Yet it was no less obvious to do such things, or their equivalents, in a former day, and it didn't happen. Back then, the dominant characteristic of philanthropy was complacency: everything was deemed to be just about as good as it could be. Now there is an urgency, a sense that philanthropy needs to catch up to a fast-changing world. And it needs to employ all the techniques at its disposal, whatever their source. That's what makes the new philanthropy so new.

CHAPTER 18

Twenty Questions — Investing in Changing the World

WHO AM I? WHAT AM I? Far more than business, philanthropy pro-vokes such questions. In philanthropy, the strategic merges with the personal. Values. Meaning. These are the raw materials out of which philanthropy is built. But what are those values, and what is the meaning? These are the questions we have devoted this book to, along with much of our lives. To pull such abstractions out of the hard business of philanthropy, we have come up with twenty questions. It's a fitting way to draw this book ever nearer to a close. These are the thoughts we would like to leave you with. And they are thoughts about you, for philanthropy is about you. You can answer the questions alone or with your family, although we suspect that you would come up with more honest answers alone:

1. How can I balance the competing impulses of looking good, feeling good, and doing good? When I am completely honest with myself, which one would I weight most heavily?

2. Have I thought about a personal mission statement or ethical will that I want to leave as a reflection of my search for meaning? If so, what is the gist of it? Have I written it down? Will it inform my philanthropic giving?

3. What is the extent of my edifice complex? To what degree do I wish to put up buildings and capital structures that bear my name?

4. Would I rather support interesting projects or quality institutions?

5. Am I a venture philanthropist? Do I want to provide risk capital for an untried program, knowing that it may fail? Or would I prefer to stick to safer projects that are more likely to succeed?

6. Do I want partners? Would I rather leverage my philanthropy with them and cede control to such a partnership, or go my own way?

7. How much do I want to be hands-on? Would I rather invest in organizations and people and monitor their progress from a distance, or do I want to be engaged in the operation?

8. Am I mission driven or market driven? Am I bent on changing the world or on flourishing?

9. Is my philanthropy an extension of "my charity"? That is, do I want to help the neediest and most vulnerable in society? Or would I prefer there be other beneficiaries of my philanthropy?

10. Do I want to be on the cutting edge of issues, approaches, and methods, despite the investment risk, or am I oriented more toward the tried and true?

11. How much fun do I want to have? Do I want to see and feel the impact of my philanthropy, or is it okay to benefit society in some less tangible way?

12. Who are my heroes? What would they advise me about my philanthropy at this time?
13. What is my exit strategy? Do I want my philanthropy to continue in perpetuity? Through just my lifetime? Through my children's lifetime?
14. To what degree do I want to evaluate the results of my philanthropy?
15. How will I decide between competing philanthropic interests? What are my criteria?
16. Would I rather have fewer initiatives with greater impact, or more initiatives that spread my philanthropy around more broadly?
17. How much time am I prepared to give? What help will I need? From a philanthropic professional or from an administrator? Where can I get good information to guide my grant making?
18. Is this all my show? Is my spouse a partner or a sounding board? Do I want my children involved? And if so, how? As interested observers, junior partners, or full partners? Is there anyone else I'd turn to?
19. Will I focus on my community? On the United States? Or in other countries around the world, if not the entire world?
20. What do I want said about my philanthropy in my eulogy?

EPILOGUE

Why We Are Here

IN HEBREW, THERE IS NO WORD FOR CHARITY. There is only a word for righteous action, justice: *tzedaka*. No reasons to give are better than any others, but some have more personal resonance. And the Victorian notion of charity, with its implications of social obligation, indeed of pity, has never captured us as much as the ideal of righteous action, with its possibility of making a difference, making the world better. Charity is a palliative; righteous action is a cure.

Its depth and sweep derive from two core beliefs of Judaism that have moved us. The first is that every human being is created in the image of God, which means to us that everyone is of infinite value, just as God is. And the second is that when God created the world, He did not make it perfect. He left it for us to perfect over time.

The perfectibility of society is a notion that is deeply embedded in the American experiment. Tocqueville picked up on it when he toured the young country in the 1830s. But it was a product of Abrahamic thought, meaning the thought of the Jewish enlightenment, which had pervaded the Christian tradition as well, and was taken up by the founding fathers. It is evident in the mythology of Cincinnatus, the Roman farmer who left his plow to come to the aid of his country and then returned to his farm again. One might

argue that the government itself was intended to be a manifesta-
tion of the volunteer spirit, which was designed to improve the lives
of the citizenry, uplift society, and achieve that ever more perfect
union that the Constitution speaks of so fervidly in its opening
line. But it is by no means exclusively an American impulse. Like
Judaism and Christianity, Islam has also fostered a philanthropic
outlook. The Aga Khan Network, for example, is a vast philanthropic undertaking overseen by the Aga Khan, and it spreads from
Pakistan across Western Europe to as far west as Toronto.

Philanthropy is a unifying force in the world. It's the urge
to help a disabled child, train a labrador retriever to give a blind
person independence, or bring music into the schools. These are
universal impulses, our better angels.

If this book has stood for anything, it is for a reexamination of
the distinction between giving and getting. Giving is not just giving.
It is also getting: getting satisfaction, fulfillment, connection,
meaning, purpose, and dozens of other high-sounding nouns
that will no longer be abstractions once you have the experience
of making a thoughtful, well-intentioned, and significant gift of
money to a cause you heartily believe in. We wrote a few chapters
back of how philanthropy occupies a void left in the interstices
among family, government, the economy, and religion. But it
is the vacancy around religion that is the significant one. While
fundamentalist religions are thriving all around the world, the
less strident, more thoughtful communitarian systems of belief are
everywhere in retreat.

To the educated classes, religion has been withdrawing from
the central place in their lives ever since the Middle Ages, when science challenged so many of the religious verities. But philanthropy
has moved into the gap, providing a civic religion for a churchless
congregation hungering for something that is both transcen-
dent and believable. At the risk of apostasy, we can't help but

observe that philanthropists have taken for themselves some of the powers that had been ascribed only to God, chiefly the ability to make life better, to reverse ill fortune. In Jewish life, there are blessings for most of the daily activities. We get up in the morning, and we bless God for waking us up. We have breakfast, and we bless God for giving us our food. And so on. Yet there is no blessing for our philanthropy. And why? Because we can't bless God for our acting Godlike.

The best philanthropy is, like the best spirituality, something that rises up out of you. It's not laid onto you. It's a need, a desire, a quest that is best expressed as an intention. So much of life involves intentionality, a word we have returned to often in this book. It is an expression of the more thoughtful and protective aspects of human nature to think ahead, to prepare, to calculate. We are here; now how do we get there? We are in this stage; now how do we get to the next stage? In middle school, if not before, youngsters are already starting to put some thought into building the sort of résumé that will impress a college when it is time. On that basis, they are, at thirteen, trying to decide if they should work at a homeless shelter or play the tuba in the band. After college, young careerists plot their moves across the corporate battlefield with the care of generals advancing through hostile territory. Even love is subject to this sort of consideration, as passion alone is not enough. Prudent lovers recognize that a good match is likely to involve two people of overlapping backgrounds, compatibility, and complementary attributes. And so it goes through decisions about where to live, what investments to make, what house to buy, and dozens of others. None are made casually, by whim, with little thought to the big picture or what this means to them.

And so the shrewd philanthropist needs to act with intentionality too. She needs to know what she is trying to achieve, where she wants to go. You give not for today but for tomorrow, and for all the tomorrows beyond it. You need to see ahead—to be a seer, not simply to see the future, but the future you can create with your gift. Change involves the future, a different future from one that would occur otherwise. If done thoughtfully, your philanthropy can create a better future for all of us—and in so doing, for yourself, since you will have made it happen. Few other endeavors in life offer such rewards.

Philanthropy is not altruism. It is about giving to get back, and it takes self-knowledge to understand what it is you want to get back, for you and for your children, from this gift of yours. It was the psychologist Abraham Maslow who posited a hierarchy of needs, which he represented as a pyramid, with the physical needs for food, warmth, and shelter toward the bottom, and the spiritual needs for meaning, purpose, and connection toward the top. In ascending from the physical to the spiritual, the needs became more personal and individual. These aren't things that all people want; they are what you alone want. They come to reflect your distinct desires, so much so that you could identify yourself in them and by them.

This is where your soul is: in that place of transcendence, where your needs touch the sublime. In many faiths, our souls live on after our death, not as ghosts but as animating spirits that enliven the memories of our friends and descendents and make us, through them, immortal. And so does our philanthropy. It is best if it is done right, with measurement, leverage, sustainability, and all the other qualities that characterize the new philanthropy. But first it needs to be done. More than our other acts in this world, our philanthropy will live on after us, reshaping the world in our image, and leaving behind a legacy that is the lasting record that we were here. We lived.

PART FOUR

Resources

"Your generous contribution helps fund these solicitations."

RESOURCE A

Index of Nonprofit Resources

A RANGE OF INFORMATION ON NONPROFITS is presented in this resource under the following topics:

- Who helps all foundations
- Who helps philanthropy as a whole
- Who helps family foundations
- Who helps community foundations
- Who helps corporate foundations and giving programs
- Who helps international grant makers
- Who helps foundations work in diverse ways
- Who helps inform foundations in their grant making
- Who helps foundations be more effective
- Who helps staff do their jobs
- Who helps boards govern
- Who helps in next-generation funding
- Who writes about philanthropy and the nonprofit sector— periodicals
- Who teaches about the nonprofit sector—academic programs

We gratefully acknowledge the assistance of the Council on Foundations, as many resources contained here come directly from its Web site (www.cof.org). For foundations, membership in the Council on Foundations and other infrastructure organizations represents a strategic combination of good philanthropic citizenship and excellent member services.

Who Helps All Foundations

Council on Foundations (www.cof.org). The national membership association for foundations and corporate giving programs
serves the public good by promoting and enhancing responsible
and effective philanthropy. It provides the field with national
conferences, critical resources, and individual assistance.

Forum of Regional Associations of Grantmakers (www.giving
forum.org). A membership association of the nation's largest
regional associations of grant makers, the forum promotes
expanded, effective philanthropy by enhancing the capacity of
regional associations of grant makers. Regional associations are
nonprofit membership associations of foundations and related
organizations that share a common goal: to strengthen philanthropy in a distinct geographical region—city, state, or multistate
area. Regional association members include private or independent
foundations, community foundations, and corporate foundations
and giving programs. In addition, some regional associations
include in their membership other related organizations, such as
financial advisor firms or nonprofit grant-seeking groups.

Philanthropy Roundtable (www.philanthropyroundtable.org).
This national membership association is founded on the principles
that voluntary private action offers the best means of addressing
society's needs and that a vibrant private sector is critical to
creating the wealth that makes philanthropy possible.

Who Helps Philanthropy as a Whole

BBB Wise Giving Alliance (www.give.org). The alliance provides
reporting and advisory service about national and international

fundraising, as well as nonprofit organizations that solicit contributions from the public. Its purpose is to maintain sound standards in the field of philanthropy and to aid wise giving through advisory reports to contributors. The alliance is a merger of the National Charities Information Bureau and the Council of Better Business Bureau Foundation and its Philanthropic Advisory Service.

Charity Navigator (www.charitynavigator.org). This is the nation's largest and most-used evaluator of charities. In an effort to help donors make informed decisions, its professional analysts have developed an unbiased, objective, numbers-based rating system to assess the financial health of over five thousand of America's best-known charities. Charity Navigator creates evaluations that are easy to understand and available to the public free of charge in an effort to advance a more efficient and responsive philanthropic marketplace.

The Foundation Center (www.foundationcenter.org). This is an essential resource for grant seekers looking for information on appropriate funding sources for their programs and organizations. It focuses on furthering public understanding of foundations by conducting research in the field.

GuideStar (www.guidestar.org). GuideStar is the operating name and registered trademark of Philanthropic Research, a 501(c)3 public charity located in Williamsburg, Virginia. Its mission is to revolutionize philanthropy and nonprofit practice with information. To that end, GuideStar has created and is constantly updating a database of information on all IRS-recognized 501(c) nonprofit organizations eligible to receive tax-deductible contributions.

Independent Sector (www.independentsector.org). The mission of this nonprofit coalition of more than 850 corporate, foundation, and voluntary organizations is to create a national forum to encourage giving and volunteering by individuals and organizations.

Indiana University Center on Philanthropy (www.philanthropy .iupui.edu). This academic center is dedicated to increasing the understanding of philanthropy and improving its practice through research, teaching, and public service.

National Committee for Responsive Philanthropy (www.ncrp .org). NCRP works with leaders in the philanthropic community and the recipients of giving to increase public accountability by philanthropies. It conducts research, compiles statistics, and publicizes reports in the philanthropic field.

Who Helps Family Foundations

21/64 (www.2164.net). This nonprofit consulting division of the Andrea and Charles Bronfman Philanthropies specializes in intergenerational philanthropy, values clarification, and strategic grant making. It uses a multigenerational approach to understanding "generational personalities," motivational values, and visions to help families define and achieve their individual and collective philanthropic goals across generations.

Association of Small Foundations (www.smallfoundations.org). This membership organization provides information, assistance, and workshops to foundations with few or no staff.

Council on Foundations (www.cof.org). The national membership association for foundations and corporate giving programs, the Council on Foundations has a strong commitment to family philanthropy. The Family Philanthropy Services Department provides resources and tools to help family foundations and philanthropic organizations develop and strengthen their philanthropy. Services include technical assistance, professional development, peer connections, publications, leadership opportunities, and its premier annual event: the Family Philanthropy Conference. Donors, trustees, family members, and staff can enhance their knowledge and skills and become more effective grant makers through these and other council services.

National Center for Family Philanthropy (www.ncfp.org). This national resource center focuses on matters of importance to families (with or without foundations) who are engaged in philanthropy.

Who Helps Community Foundations

Community Foundations of America (www.cfamerica.org). CFA was created in 1999 in order to offer community foundations the tools and environment to excel. Its subscribers share a collective vision about driving the development of cutting-edge services and products that advance community foundation marketing, technology, accountability, and partnerships.

Community foundation networks in the United States. The following states have local networks providing services to community foundations: Alabama, California, Florida, Georgia, Illinois, Iowa, Louisiana, Maryland, Nebraska, New York, North Carolina, Pennsylvania, South Carolina, Virginia, Washington, and West Virginia. Most Caribbean islands have these networks as well. Contact the Council on Foundations community services department for more information (community@cof.org) or call 202/466–6512.

Who Helps Corporate Foundations and Giving Programs

Association of Corporate Contributions Professionals (www .accprof.org). This nonprofit advocacy and continuing education organization helps corporations identify and adopt best practices and provides training for professionals in the contributions, community relations, and volunteerism fields.

Business Civic Leadership Center (BCLC), U.S. Chamber of Commerce (www.uschamber.com/ccc/about/default). The BCLC serves the humanitarian, philanthropic, and civic needs and aspirations of American business. It assists small and medium-sized business owners, corporate foundation and corporate community relations managers, and chamber executives.

Business for Social Responsibility (www.bsr.org). This nonprofit business association helps companies of all sizes and sectors to achieve success in ways that demonstrate respect for ethical values, people, communities, and the environment. It equips its member companies with the expertise to design and implement successful, socially responsible business policies, practices, and processes.

Center for Corporate Citizenship at Boston College (www.bc .edu/centers/ccc/index.html). This leading resource on corporate citizenship provides research, executive education, consultation, and convenings on citizenship topics. Its mission is to establish corporate citizenship as a business essential, with the goal that all companies act as economic and social assets by integrating social interests with other core business objectives.

Committee Encouraging Corporate Philanthropy (www.corpo ratephilanthropy.org). This is the only international forum of business CEOs and chairpersons pursuing a mission focused exclusively on corporate philanthropy. Its mission is to lead the business community in raising the level and quality of corporate philanthropy.

The Conference Board (www.conference-board.org). The Conference Board creates and disseminates knowledge about management and the marketplace to help businesses strengthen their performance and better serve society. It conducts research, convenes conferences, makes forecasts, assesses trends, publishes information and analysis, and brings executives together to learn from one another.

Who Helps International Grant Makers

CIVICUS (www.civicus.org). CIVICUS World Alliance for Citizen Participation is an international alliance of members in about a hundred countries who have worked for over a decade to strengthen citizen action and civil society throughout the world, especially in areas where participatory democracy and citizens' freedom of association are threatened. One of its main goals is to promote dialogue among diverse groups in society.

Council on Foundations (www.cof.org/international). International Programs at the Council on Foundations serve the public good by facilitating responsible and effective grant making for international purposes, educating the public and U.S. government about the value of international grant making, and supporting philanthropy as an essential part of a strengthened civil society around the world. The United States International Grantmakers (USIG) project is a flagship product of International Programs, available to the public (www.usig.org). USIG shares best practices, explains complex legal requirements, provides model materials for foundations to use with their overseas grantees, and advocates for more favorable government regulation of international grant making.

European Foundation Centre (www.efc.be). This international association of foundations and corporate funders is dedicated to creating and enabling the legal and fiscal environment for foundations, documenting the foundation landscape, strengthening the infrastructure of the sector, and promoting collaboration, both among foundations and between foundations and other actors, to advance the public good in Europe and beyond.

Global Philanthropists Circle (www.synergos.org/philanthropistscircle). This network of international philanthropists is organized under the Synergos Institute, an organization that supports antipoverty efforts. It provides opportunities for members to advance their own philanthropic projects by drawing on the advice, experience, relationships, and collaboration of other members. In addition, it supports initiatives to work together with international development agencies, foundations, and other philanthropic organizations.

Global Philanthropy Forum (www.philanthropyforum.org). This membership organization matches individual grant makers to vehicles for overseas giving, assists foundations and governmental donor agencies in finding partners in global philanthropy, and highlights international issues of concern. Participants are established and emerging philanthropists and social investors who seek fresh approaches to problem solving through strategic international giving and investing to advance individual opportunity and improve quality of life.

Grantmakers Without Borders (www.gwob.net). This is a network of trustees and staff of public and private foundations as well as individual donors who practice global social change philanthropy. It is a project of the Tides Center, a community foundation offering a range of infrastructure services, and a working group of the National Network of Grantmakers.

Worldwide Initiatives for Grantmaker Support (www.wings web.org). WINGS seeks to strengthen the institutional infrastructure of philanthropy worldwide by building a strong, interconnected, and collaborative global network of grant maker associations and support organizations, which helps grant-making institutions that support civil society build a more equitable and just global community. The WINGS Web site makes available a searchable database of 136 member organizations, as well as an electronic library of resources for grant-maker associations and support organizations.

Affinity resources, which assist specific interest groups in international grant making:

- Affinity Group on Japanese Philanthropy
- Africa Grantmakers Affinity Group
- Asian Americans/Pacific Islanders in Philanthropy
- Environmental Grantmakers Association
- Funders Concerned About AIDS
- Funders Network on Trade and Globalization
- Grantmakers Concerned with Immigrants and Refugees
- Hispanics in Philanthropy
- International Funders for Indigenous Peoples
- International Human Rights Funders Group
- Jewish Funders Network
- National Network of Grantmakers
- Peace and Security Funders Group

Who Helps Foundations Work in Diverse Ways

ABFE (www.abfe.org). This philanthropic partnership for black communities works to encourage increased grant making that addresses issues and problems facing African Americans and to promote the status and number of African Americans in philanthropy.

Asian Americans/Pacific Islanders in Philanthropy (www.aapip .org). AAPIP works to inform the philanthropic community about critical and emerging issues in the Asian Pacific American community; increase Asian Pacific American representation on boards of trustees and staff of philanthropic organizations; and increase the ability of Asian Pacific American nonprofits to access philanthropic funds.

Disability Funders Network (www.disabilityfunders.org). DFN works to share information on grant-making opportunities and current developments related to people with disabilities and promote the inclusion of people with disabilities in the field of philanthropy.

Emerging Practitioners in Philanthropy (www.epip.org). The mission of EPIP is to strengthen the next generation of grant makers in order to advance effective social justice philanthropy.

Foundations and Donors Interested in Catholic Activities (www.fadica.org). FADICA is a consortium of private charitable foundations and individual donors who share an interest in religious philanthropy. The organization functions primarily as a learning and leadership forum for its members. It enables its members to track trends and research of significance to faith-based philanthropy, interact with religious leaders, help solve problems, and mentor the next generation of foundation trustees.

Funders for Lesbian and Gay Issues (www.lgbtfunders.org). The mission of this organization is to increase the philanthropic community's knowledge and understanding of critical funding needs in lesbian, gay, bisexual, and transgender communities and to educate lesbian and gay organizations on how to access philanthropic resources.

The Gathering (www.gatheringweb.com). The Gathering holds conferences or forums for individuals, families, or their foundations that give a minimum of $200,000 annually to Christian ministries or have the capacity to do so. The Gathering is also open to staff and trustees of foundations, but Gathering activities are not open to staff of ministries (except by invitation).

Hispanics in Philanthropy (www.hiponline.org). Hispanics in Philanthropy advocates for increased philanthropic support of Latino communities and greater representation of Latinos on the boards and staff of foundations.

Jewish Funders Network (www.jfunders.org). JFN is an organization of individual and institutional grant makers committed to broadening the base and scope of Jewish philanthropy and advancing its effective practice. To respond to the challenges of the twenty-first century and the evolving needs of the Jewish community, it seeks to provide a forum for exposing the broadest range of contemporary creative and innovative thinking, foster growth and vitality in Jewish charitable giving, encourage informed grant making to Jewish and secular causes that embody Jewish values, and facilitate cooperation and partnerships among grant makers.

Joint Affinity Groups (e-mail: info@jointaffinitygroups.org). JAG is a coalition of grant-maker associations that engages the field of philanthropy to reach its full potential by supporting diversity, inclusiveness, and the principles of social justice and promoting a more equitable distribution of resources. It exemplifies the broad meaning of *diversity* that is inclusive of sexual orientation and identity and disability. JAG is dedicated to the principle of accountability to one another and to all of the communities it serves. It strives to advance the principles of social justice in philanthropy and the nonprofit sector through convenings, educational programs, and research. JAG uses a virtual operating structure. Representatives from each member group participate in a steering committee, which accomplishes the planning and ongoing work. A coordinating committee comprising three JAG members manages the work. Consultants are hired for specific projects.

National Center for Black Philanthropy (www.ncfbp.net). NCBP was established to promote giving and volunteerism among African Americans, foster full participation by African Americans in all aspects of philanthropy, educate the public about the contributions of black philanthropy, strengthen people and institutions engaged in black philanthropy, and research the benefits of black philanthropy to all Americans. It conducts several programs, chief among which are national and regional conferences on black philanthropy.

Native Americans in Philanthropy (www.nativephilanthropy .org). NAP works to increase the understanding and presence of organized philanthropy in Native communities and to serve as a bridge between Native people and organized philanthropy.

Women & Philanthropy (www.womenphil.org). Women & Philanthropy provides leadership for foundations and philanthropy to create a more caring and just world through the full engagement of women and girls.

Women's Funding Network (www.wfnet.org). The mission of WFN, a partnership of women's funds, donors, and allies around the world committed to social justice, is to ensure that women's funds are recognized as the investment of choice for people who value the full participation of women and girls as key to strong, equitable, and sustainable communities and societies.

Who Helps Inform Foundations in Their Grant Making

Arts, Culture, and Humanities

Grantmakers in the Arts (www.giarts.org). Grantmakers in the Arts works to strengthen arts philanthropy and its role in contributing to a supportive environment for the arts nationwide.

Grantmakers in Film and Electronic Media (www.gfem.org). GFEM works to promote awareness and understanding of the ways "motion media" (film, television, video, and the newer digital technologies such as CD-ROM and the Web) can enhance effective grant making.

Education

Grantmakers for Education (www.edfunders.org). This membership organization for private and public grant makers supports education from early childhood through K–12 and higher education. Its mission is to improve educational outcomes for students by strengthening philanthropic capability and effectiveness.

Environment

Environmental Grantmakers Association (www.ega.org). EGA is a voluntary association of foundations and giving programs concerned with protecting the natural environment.

Health

Funders Concerned About AIDS (www.fcaaids.org). This organization mobilizes philanthropic leadership and resources, domestically and internationally, to eradicate the HIV/AIDS pandemic and address its social and economic consequences.

Funders Network on Population, Reproductive Health & Rights (www.fundersnet.org). The mission of this group is to ensure that all people have access to the information and services they need to manage their own fertility and protect and promote their sexual and reproductive health.

Grantmakers in Health (www.gih.org). GIH is a nonprofit educational organization serving trustees and staff of foundations and corporate giving programs. Its mission is to help grant makers improve the nation's health by strengthening their knowledge, skills, and effectiveness and fostering communication and collaboration among grant makers and with others.

Human Services

Coalition of Community Foundations for Youth (www.ccfy .org). The coalition's mission is to strengthen the leadership capacity of community foundations to improve the lives of children, youth, and families.

Grantmakers in Aging (www.giaging.org). GIA works to promote and strengthen grant making for an aging society. It is an educational organization for staff and trustees of foundations and corporate foundations and giving programs that enables its members to network with other funders in aging, gain tools to make excellent aging grants, acquire information about the needs of the elderly as well as the resources they bring to their communities, receive updates about trends and policy changes affecting older adults, learn about current and upcoming funding initiatives in aging, and link to other sources of information in the field of aging.

Grantmakers for Children, Youth & Families (www.gcyf.org). GCYF works to promote awareness and action around children, youth, and family issues in philanthropy; strengthen the knowledge and use of available resources; and serve as a point of contact for those seeking collegial and collaborative relationships with other grant makers concerned with children, youth, and families.

Grantmakers Concerned with Immigrants and Refugees (www .gcir.org). GCIR works to promote awareness and understanding among funders about issues concerning newcomers, immigration, refugee trends, and public policy; facilitate the sharing of information on these issues among grant makers; and increase financial support for projects and activities concerned with immigrants and refugees.

Neighborhood Funders Group (www.nfg.org). NFG is a membership association of grant-making institutions. Its mission is to strengthen the capacity of organized philanthropy to understand and support community-based efforts to organize and improve the economic and social fabric of low-income urban neighborhoods and rural communities. It provides information, learning opportunities, and other professional development activities to its national membership, and encourages the support of policies and practices that advance economic and social justice.

International/Foreign Affairs

Africa Grantmakers' Affinity Group (www.africagrantmakers .org). AGAG aims to encourage increased and more effective foundation funding in Africa by improving networking opportunities and enhancing collaboration, capacity-building opportunities, and linkages among new and experienced donors.

Grantmakers Concerned with Immigrants and Refugees (www .gcir.org). GCIR works to promote awareness and understanding among funders about issues concerning newcomers, immigration, refugee trends, and public policy; facilitate the sharing of information on these issues among grant makers; and increase financial support for projects and activities concerned with immigrants and refugees.

Grantmakers Without Borders (www.internationaldonors.org *or* www.gwob.net). This joint project of the International Donors' Dialogue and the International Working Group of the National Network of Grantmakers seeks to increase philanthropic funding outside the United States. It offers information and free consultation about international grant-making opportunities.

International Funders for Indigenous People (www.internation alfunders.org). IFIP works to provide a venue for communications and resource sharing among international funders of indigenous peoples.

International Human Rights Funders Group (www.hrfunders .org). This group is an association of grant makers devoted to supporting efforts to achieve the rights enshrined in the Universal Declaration of Human Rights and the treaties it has generated so that all people may enjoy a truly and fully human existence.

Peace and Security Funders Group (www.peaceandsecurity.org). This group is dedicated to enhancing the effectiveness of philanthropy to promote international peace security. To this end, it provides opportunities for education and information sharing, facilitates the development of effective strategies and collaborations, and encourages greater and new investments in this challenging and rewarding area of work.

Public and Society Benefit

Alliance for Justice (www.afj.org). This is a national association of environmental, civil rights, mental health, women's, children's, and consumer advocacy organizations. Since its inception in 1979, it has worked to advance the cause of justice for all Americans, strengthen the public interest community's ability to influence public policy, and foster the next generation of advocates.

Funders' Network for Smart Growth and Livable Communities (www.fundersnetwork.org). Its mission is to strengthen funders' individual and collective abilities to support organizations promoting smart growth and livable communities.

Grantmakers Income Security Taskforce (www.gistfunders.org). GIST promotes understanding of income security issues among funders and seeks to advance collaborative strategies in this area.

Grassroots Grantmakers (www.grassrootsgrantmakers.org). This group connects and supports funding organizations that are engaged in grassroots grant making. This work is designed to strengthen resident-controlled associations and help people come together because of a shared interest in improving their block, neighborhood, or community and becoming stronger voices for change. It is also interested in learning about how funders use other tools, such as convening, technical assistance, training, and leadership development, to support bottom-up community building.

National Network of Grantmakers (www.nng.org). NNG is an organization of individuals involved in funding social and economic justice. The network values individuals, projects, and organizations working for systemic change in the United States and abroad in order to create an equitable distribution of wealth and power with mutual respect for all peoples. It works primarily within organized philanthropy to increase financial and other resources to groups committed to social and economic justice.

Neighborhood Funders Group (www.nfg.org). NFG is a national network of foundations and philanthropic organizations whose members support community-based efforts that improve economic and social conditions in low-income communities. The group provides information, learning opportunities, critical thinking, and other professional development activities to its members.

PACE: Philanthropy for Active Civic Engagement (www.pace funders.org). PACE inspires interest, understanding, and investment in civic engagement. It aims to build a community within philanthropy committed to debate and action around encouraging participation and engagement in community, civic, and political life. It aims to inspire and incubate strategic collaborations with policymakers, nonprofits, business, and the media to support active citizenship.

Who Helps Foundations Be More Effective

Alliance for Nonprofit Management (www.allianceonline.org). The alliance is a professional association devoted to improving management and governance among nonprofit organizations.

Center for Effective Philanthropy (www.effectivephilanthropy .org). CEP is a nonprofit organization focused on the development of comparative data to enable higher-performing funders.

Its mission is to provide data and create insight so philanthropic funders can better define, assess, and improve their effectiveness and impact. It pursues its mission through data collection and research that fuel the creation of assessment tools, publications, and programming. CEP has produced widely referenced research reports on foundation performance assessment, foundation strategy, foundation governance, and foundation-grantee relationships. It has created new data sets relevant to foundation leaders and hosts highly regarded programming focused on key issues related to funder effectiveness.

Grantmakers for Effective Organizations (www.geofunders.org). GEO works to promote learning and dialogue about the effectiveness of nonprofit organizations, the wide range of strategies for accomplishing organization building, and the constructive and catalytic roles funders can play in encouraging and supporting organizational effectiveness among nonprofits.

Innovation Network (www.innonet.org). InnoNet helps nonprofit organizations build evaluation knowledge and skills, strengthen the capacity to improve and learn through the use of participatory evaluation, and embrace and implement change.

Who Helps Staff Do Their Jobs

Association of Fundraising Professionals (www.afpnet.org). AFP represents more than twenty-seven thousand members in 180 chapters throughout the United States, Canada, Mexico, and China working to advance philanthropy through advocacy, research, education, and certification programs. It is committed to preparing its members, the profession, and the sector to respond to the challenges of a dynamic philanthropic environment.

The Communications Network (www.comnetwork.org). The network promotes communications as an essential and integral component of grant making. In support of that mission, it provides leadership on the strategic role of communications in philanthropy, expands and enhances the communications capacity of grant makers, and offers grant makers the services and resources to communicate more effectively both internally and externally.

Consortium of Foundation Libraries (www.foundationlibraries .org). The CFL is a vehicle for enhancing learning, sharing resources, and coordinating information services among foundation libraries and archives.

Foundation Financial Officer's Group (www.ffog.org). FFOG is a nonprofit membership organization of financial and investment officers of large, private foundations in the United States and abroad (defined as those with at least $200 million in assets).

Giving Institute (www.aafrc.org). The Giving Institute publishes *Giving USA,* the annual yearbook on American philanthropy, and supports research and education. It continues to provide financial support, expertise, and leadership to the foundation world and works in partnership with foundations to advance philanthropy and promote ethics in the fundraising profession.

GrantCraft (www.grantcraft.org). This is a source of practical wisdom for grant makers on the tools and techniques of effective grant making. It offers guides, videos, and case studies that present the practitioner's view of philanthropy.

Grants Managers Network (www.gmnetwork.org). GMN provides a forum to exchange information about grants management and its relevance to efficient and effective grant making. It is an affinity group of the Council on Foundations and a project of the Rockefeller Family Fund. It currently has a thousand members representing more than seven hundred private, community, and corporate foundations.

Technology Affinity Group (www.tagtech.org). TAG is a technology forum for professionals working in philanthropy. It seeks to advance best practices in technology through a network of technical and nontechnical foundation staff.

Who Helps Boards Govern

BoardSource (www.boardsource.org). This international association focuses on strengthening the effectiveness of nonprofit governing boards by providing information, resources, and consulting services.

Trustee Leadership Development (www.tld.org). TLD's mission is to develop ethical and responsible individual and organizational leadership capable of reaching the greatest potential and of contributing to the common good.

Who Helps in Next-Generation Funding

21/64 (www.2164.net). 21/64 is a nonprofit consulting division of the Andrea and Charles Bronfman Philanthropies specializing in intergenerational philanthropy, values clarification, and strategic grant making. It uses a multigenerational approach to understanding generational personalities, motivational values, and visions to help families define and achieve their individual and collective goals across generations.

Resource Generation (www.resourcegeneration.org). Resource Generation offers a variety of programs for young people with wealth to explore how their financial resources relate to social justice and provides tools for them to take action. It offers forums to promote cross-class and intergenerational dialogues about money, class, and philanthropy.

Leverage Alliance (www.leval.org). Seeks to grow a global community of the next generation of leaders who have significant financial resources, in which they share knowledge, networks, and vision and build alliances for specific projects in order to achieve a greater, more systematic positive social impact on the world.

Youth on Board (www.youthonboard.org). Youth on Board prepares youth to be leaders in their communities and strengthen relationships between youth and adults by providing publications, customized workshops, and technical assistance.

Youth Leadership Institute (www.yli.org). YLI builds communities where young people and their adult allies come together to create positive social change. It designs and implements community-based programs that provide youth with leadership skills in the areas of drug and alcohol abuse prevention, philanthropy, and civic engagement. Building on these real-world program experiences, it creates curricula and training programs that foster social change efforts across the nation, all while promoting best practices in the field of youth development.

Who Writes About Philanthropy and the Nonprofit Sector — Periodicals

Advancing Philanthropy. Published bimonthly by the Association of Fundraising Professionals, *Advancing Philanthropy* is an idea and strategy magazine for fundraisers in all sectors. With detailed reports and analyses of current trends, it educates, informs, and challenges the development community, giving readers practical applications and how-to articles, new research, interviews with donors, and tips and ideas from peers in the fundraising profession. http://www.afpnet.org/publications/advancing_philanthropy

Alliance Magazine. A monthly magazine providing news and analysis of what's happening in the philanthropy and social investment sectors across the world. It also acts as a forum for exchange of ideas and experiences among practitioners. As well as news and conference reports, articles, book reviews, and opinion columns, each issue has a special in-depth feature on a key aspect of philanthropy and social investment, with contributors from around the world and expert guest editors. www.alliancemagazine.org

Associations Now. A monthly magazine for association executives published by the American Society of Association Executives and the Center for Association Leadership. It delivers essential information and ideas that empower associations to master challenges, invoke imagination, and act decisively to create a better world. The January issue is devoted to addressing the needs of boards and other volunteer leaders. ASAE also publishes the *Journal of Association Leadership,* the only peer-reviewed journal for the association profession. www.asaecenter.org/publicationsresources/

BBB Wise Giving Guide. A quarterly magazine published by the BBB Wise Giving Alliance. It includes a summary of the latest results of the alliance's national charity evaluations, along with a cover story about giving tips or charity accountability issues. www.bbb.org/charity

BoardSource. This electronic newsletter features news and resources for nonprofit leaders (for members only). www.board source.org

Chronicle of Philanthropy. The newspaper of the nonprofit world, it features news and information for charity leaders, fundraisers, grant makers, and others involved in the philanthropic enterprise. A subscription to the biweekly publication includes full access to the Web site database and news updates by e-mail. An online-only subscription is also available. www.philanthropy.com

Contributions. The how-to magazine for those working at America's charitable organizations, *Contributions* focuses on all facets of fundraising and organizational management. Each issue offers executive directors and development officers a wealth of articles, information, and tips on subjects such as board development, major gifts fundraising, prospect and donor research, direct mail fundraising, volunteer management, nonprofit marketing, Internet and e-mail fundraising, proposal writing, planned giving, and corporate and foundation fundraising. www.contributions magazine.com

Corporate Philanthropist. The Committee Encouraging Corporate Philanthropy's quarterly publication, newly branded the *Corporate Philanthropist,* features best practices and perspectives on corporate philanthropy from CEO members and industry thought leaders. http://www.corporatephilanthropy.org/ncp/

Council on Foundations. The Council on Foundations (www .cof.org) publishes a variety of electronic newsletters addressing topics of interest to the grant-making community:

Breaking News—national and regional media coverage of philanthropy and the charitable sector every morning by e- mail. Public Relations department, 703/879–0679 media@cof.org

Thought > Action > Impact. Published bimonthly, this thought journal gives voice to some of the most influential leaders from the public, private, and nonprofit sectors on timely topics. TAI offers grant makers both philosophical perspectives and practical advice relevant to the philanthropic field. www.cofinteract.org/taijournal

The following are available to members as a benefit of Council on Foundations membership:

CFSource—a monthly newsletter for community foundations. Community Foundation Services department, CFSource@ cof.org

Corporate Update—a monthly newsletter with the latest information for corporate grant makers. Corporate Grantmaking Services department, 703/879–0737, corpserv@cof.org

Family Matters—a quarterly update of family philanthropy news, articles, and events. Family Philanthropy Services, family@ cof.org

International Dateline—a monthly review of news, interviews with notable international grant makers, and information for international grant makers. International Programs, internationalprograms@cof.org/

Washington Quarterly—an electronic publication informing readers about legislative and regulatory developments; available to council members and Philanthropic Advisors Network subscribers. Public Policy and Research department, govt@ cof.org/

Effect Magazine. The European Foundation Centre's flagship publication about and for European foundations, with an emphasis on its members. The magazine, published three times per year, covers foundations' impact and role in Europe and the rest of the world; operational issues; the political, legal, and fiscal environments in which foundations work; and how they get that work done, both individually and in collaboration with others. www.efc.be/publications/effect.htm

Forbes. Focuses on top management and those aspiring to positions of corporate leadership in business. It provides information on successful companies and individuals, industries, marketing, law, taxes, technology, computers, communications, investments, and management performance, and it includes a column on philanthropy in its Personal Finance section. www.forbes.com/finance/philanthropy/

FundRaising Success. A practical guide for nonprofit organizations, founded in 2003. It exists to help development staffs raise money for and interest in their organizations' missions. Encyclopedic in its approach, it covers everything from e-philanthropy and direct mail to donor retention and regulatory issues. http://www.fundraisingsuccessmag.com/

Grantsmanship Center Magazine. The Grantsmanship Center publications contain information on how to plan, manage, staff, and fund the programs of nonprofit organizations and government agencies. *The Grantsmanship Center News,* also called *Grantsmanship Center Magazine,* has reached over 200,000 nonprofit and government agencies at its peak. These periodicals "paved the way for the journalists who today scrutinize charities and foundations with growing sophistication and skepticism," according to the *Chronicle of Philanthropy.* Although no longer in print, these publications continue to provide superb historical frameworks for nonprofit management. Archives are available at the Library of Congress and online at www.tgci.com/magazine.shtml.

Grassroots Fundraising Journal. Published bimonthly by the Grassroots Institute for Fundraising Training, a multiracial organization that promotes the connection between fundraising, social justice, and movement building. This journal was cofounded in 1981 by Kim Klein and Lisa Honig, who saw that most of the resources on nonprofit fundraising are not applicable to grassroots groups, especially those challenging and changing the status quo. The journal provides organizations with affordable and practical information and ideas for fundraising. www.grassroots fundraising.org

Inspire Your World. The first consumer magazine dedicated to volunteerism, bringing together community leaders, celebrities, CEOS, and everyday people who share a common commitment to giving back. *Inspire Your World* serves as a primary source for news on the nonprofit industry and on companies and individuals dedicated to volunteerism, philanthropy, and community service. Its mission is to generate pathways to action that increase volunteerism and giving by illustrating how companies, nonprofit organizations, and individuals work together to meet the needs of the communities they serve. www.inspireyourworld.com

Journal for Nonprofit Management. The *Journal,* published by the Support Center for Nonprofit Management, is an annual publication for those concerned with developing excellence in nonprofit management. It is a source of thinking and articles on the issues challenging nonprofit organizations today. www.support ctr.org/resources.php

Nonprofit and Voluntary Sector Quarterly. NVSQ, the journal of the Association for Research on Nonprofit Organizations and Voluntary Action, is dedicated to enhancing our knowledge of nonprofit organizations, philanthropy, and voluntarism by providing cutting-edge research, discussion, and analysis of the field and leads its readers to understand the impact the nonprofit sector has on society. It provides a forum for researchers from around the world to publish timely articles from a variety of disciplinary perspectives. http://nvs.sagepub.com/

Nonprofit Board Report. A newsletter offering short articles to help nonprofit executives and boards work together more effectively. Every monthly issue tackles issues that nonprofit organizations regularly struggle with, for example, making board members better fundraisers and improving the relationship between the executive director and the board. The newsletter offers strategies for fundraising, recruiting board members, helping board members understand their roles, and solving management and financial planning problems. http://www.pbp.com/nbreport.html

Nonprofit Quarterly. A national journal whose overarching editorial goal is to strengthen the role of nonprofit organizations to activate democracy. The journal is committed to providing a forum for the critical thinking and exploration needed to help nonprofits stay true to this democratic calling and to achieve their potential as effective, powerful, and influential organizations in concert with their constituencies. www.nonprofitquarterly.org

Nonprofit World Magazine. A bimonthly magazine published since 1983 that provides nonprofit leaders with concise and practical articles whose advice can be easily implemented. *Nonprofit World* is published by the Society for Nonprofit Organizations, which provides nonprofit staff members, volunteers, and board members with resources and information to work more effectively and efficiently toward accomplishing their mission. www.snpo.org/publications/nonprofitworld.php

The Nonprofit Times. Published twice a month, this publication provides useful information on the business of managing nonprofit organizations. Free subscriptions are offered to full-time U.S. nonprofit executives. www.nptimes.com

The Philanthropist. A quarterly journal for managers, directors, and legal and financial advisors of Canadian charitable organizations and foundations. It publishes articles and information relevant to the Canadian philanthropic sector and provides a forum for discussion and informed debate of controversial issues arising in this sector. www.thephilanthropist.ca/

Philanthropy. Published by the Philanthropy Roundtable, this six-times-a-year publication offers coverage and commentary on issues of concern to donors, featuring interviews with philanthropists and advice on foundation management. http://philanthropy roundtable.org/

Philanthropy Matters Magazine. A semiannual magazine that provides professionals and volunteers with quick and easy access to ideas and news. Each issue contains practical, need-to-know results from the latest research conducted by faculty and staff at the Center on Philanthropy at Indiana University and by other practitioners and scholars around the world. www.philanthropy .iupui.edu/Research/PhilanthropyMatters/

Philanthropy World Magazine. Celebrates the philanthropic spirit in the United States and around the globe. Published six times a year, it features articles on extraordinary people who are dedicated to charitable causes. In addition, each issue highlights areas of philanthropic giving, such as corporate giving, foundations, and volunteering, as well as key nonprofit agencies and contributors. The magazine publishes information that keeps readers up-to-date on the latest important philanthropic happenings around the country and the rest of the world. www.philanthropymagazine.com

Responsive Philanthropy. Published quarterly by the National Committee for Responsive Philanthropy, *Responsive Philanthropy* provides comprehensive coverage of trends and critical issues surrounding foundation, corporate, and workplace philanthropy as they affect social justice and the public interest. www.ncrp.org/publications/index.asp

Stanford Social Innovation Review. Published quarterly by the Stanford Graduate School of Business, the review's mission is to share substantive insights and practical experiences that will help those who do the work of improving society do it even better. The main audience is nonprofit executives, grant-making executives, social entrepreneurs, and corporate executives concerned with social, environmental, and community issues. The *Review* aims to foster an exchange of views among the public, nonprofit, and private sectors, focusing on advancing strategic management and leadership in the social sector. www.ssireview.org

Trust and Foundation News. The Association of Charitable Foundations' quarterly magazine is packed with news, views, and information and provides up-to-date briefings on issues in grant making in the United Kingdom. www.acf.org.uk/publicationsandresources/

***VOLUNTAS*: International Journal of Voluntary and Non-profit Organizations.** *VOLUNTAS* is published on behalf of the International Society for Third-Sector Research, a major international association promoting research and education in the fields of civil society, philanthropy, and the nonprofit sector. The association is dedicated to the creation, discussion, and advancement of knowledge pertaining to the third sector and its impact on human and planetary well-being and development internationally. www.istr.org

Worth. Aimed at high-net-worth individuals and their advisors, *Worth* reports on issues related to comprehensive wealth management, including investment opportunities (for example, alternative investments, private equity, hedge funds, and real estate), private banking and financial advisory services, business ownership and succession planning, as well as philanthropy and estate planning. www.worth.com

Who Teaches About the Nonprofit Sector—Academic Programs

Columbia University Business School, Institute for Not-for-Profit Management (www4.gsb.columbia.edu/execed/inm). For over thirty years, the Institute for Not-for-Profit Management at Executive Education at Columbia Business School has equipped nonprofit and public sector organizations to be ready to meet the challenges of today's fast-paced and dynamic environments. Through intensive graduate-level programs, participants study core management disciplines tailored to the nonprofit sector. Students in this program learn to develop and use scarce resources, manage growth and competition, and serve their constituents.

Harvard University, Hauser Center for Nonprofit Organizations, John F. Kennedy School of Government (www.hks .harvard.edu/hauser). The Hauser Center seeks to expand understanding of and accelerate critical thinking about civil society among scholars, practitioners, policymakers, and the general public by encouraging scholarship, developing curriculum, fostering mutual learning between academics and practitioners, and shaping policies that enhance the sector and its role in society. It strives to explore the critical questions affecting nonprofits, support teaching about nonprofit organizations across Harvard University, develop curricula in the field, and connect current and future leaders with new thinking and scholarship.

Indiana University, Center on Philanthropy (www.philanthropy .iupui.edu). The center pioneered philanthropic studies as an academic subject, exploring and explaining both the theory and practice of how and why philanthropy works. Offering master's and doctoral degrees in philanthropic studies as well as lifelong learning opportunities, the center applies a liberal arts approach that studies and teaches the subject from a variety of disciplines using qualitative and quantitative approaches. The Center on Philanthropy is a leading academic center dedicated to increasing the understanding of philanthropy, improving its practice, and enhancing participation in philanthropy through research, teaching, public service, and public affairs programs in philanthropy, fundraising, and management of nonprofit organizations.

Johns Hopkins University Center for Civil Society Studies, Institute for Policy Studies (www.jhu.edu/~ccss/). The Center for Civil Society Studies seeks to improve understanding and the effective functioning of nonprofit, philanthropic, and civil society organizations in the United States and throughout the rest of the world in order to enhance the contribution these organizations can make to democracy and the quality of human life. The center is part of the Johns Hopkins Institute for Policy Studies and carries out its work through a combination of research, training, and information sharing both domestically and internationally. The institute features a distinguished staff of policy professionals covering economic development, housing and urban policy, human resource development policy, and many other major social issues.

Maxwell School of Syracuse University, Campbell Public Affairs Institute (www.maxwell.syr.edu/campbell). The Nonprofit Studies Program was established under the auspices of the Campbell Public Affairs Institute to create and facilitate sharing of knowledge about nonprofit governance, management, and policy. Its mission is to examine the ideal of citizenship, its evolution, and the conditions under which it thrives. The program ties together nonprofit research, outreach, and teaching activities to explore the relationship among citizens, private organizations, and government in an effort to improve understanding of the development and implementation of effective leadership, management, and policy.

New York University, Heyman Center for Philanthropy and Fundraising, School of Continuing & Professional Studies (www.scps.nyu.edu/areas-of-study/philanthropy-fundraising/).
The Heyman Center is one of the preeminent educators of fundraisers and grant makers, offering a solid foundation in the field while helping students develop their own fundraising philosophy and framework through advanced study of the history and theory of the industry. The Heyman Center offerings include graduate level and certificate coursework in grant making, foundations, and fundraising for nonprofit, corporate, and foundation practitioners, executives, and volunteers.

New York University, Robert F. Wagner Graduate School of Public Service (http://wagner.nyu.edu). Established in 1938, the Robert F. Wagner Graduate School of Public Service offers advanced programs that educate future leaders of public, nonprofit, and health institutions as well as private organizations serving the public sector. Trained in management, policy, and finance, Wagner students graduate with the skills they need to confront society's most pressing problems. NYU Wagner offers a dynamic approach to preparing people to serve the public through education, research, and service. It delivers a practical approach with an urban focus and global perspective.

Northwestern University Kellogg School of Management Center for Nonprofit Management (www.kellogg.northwestern .edu/research/nonprofit/index.htm). Founded in 1998, the center's mission is to become an internationally recognized resource in the field of nonprofit management education and higher education through graduate degree and executive management programs. The center aims to harness the resources of the Kellogg School of Management at Northwestern University to partner with the nonprofit community. It relies on both academic faculty and practitioners from various areas of the nonprofit sector to form a bridge between the academic community and the nonprofit sector.

Stanford University Graduate School of Business, Center for Social Innovation (www.gsb.stanford.edu/csi). The Graduate School of Business believes that business schools have a responsibility to teach students to be innovative, principled, and insightful leaders who can change the world. As such, the center represents a cornerstone of the school's multidisciplinary approach to management and leadership education. The center invests its resources in an integrated set of activities that are designed to enhance the leadership and management capacity of individuals who strive to create social and environmental value. Through the discovery and worldwide dissemination of new ideas, it increases awareness of social problems and provides frameworks for thinking about and solving these problems.

University of California at Berkeley, Center for Nonprofit and Public Leadership (http://groups.haas.berkeley.edu/nonprofit). The center prepares leaders with practical business skills to found, lead, manage, and govern nonprofit and public organizations for the public good. It provides M.B.A. students an opportunity to augment the core business curriculum with specialized course work, practical application, and career opportunities in public and nonprofit management.

University of Southern California School of Policy, Planning and Development Center on Philanthropy and Public Policy (www.usc.edu/schools/sppd/philanthropy). The Center on Philanthropy and Public Policy acts as a catalyst for understanding and action at the intersection of the public, private, and nonprofit sectors by providing information and analysis of value to decision makers in the three sectors. The master of public administration program reflects both the breadth and diversity of the ever-changing nature of public administration. Through research and communications, the center provides information about the changing philanthropic landscape, profiles the resulting challenges for the sector and for society, and stimulates conversation to foster understanding and to advance public problem solving.

UCLA Center for Civil Society (www.spa.ucla.edu/ccs). The Center for Civil Society is the focal point for UCLA's School of Public Affairs programs in nonprofit leadership and management, grassroots advocacy, nongovernmental organizations, and philanthropy. It coordinates teaching on nonprofit organizations and aspects of civil society; conducts research; and offers seminars, conferences, colloquia, and executive education as part of community engagement. In undertaking these mutually supporting activities, it seeks to contribute to the policy dialogue on the current and future role of nonprofit organizations, philanthropy, and civil society.

RESOURCE B

Further Sources
of Information

FOR ADDITIONAL INFORMATION ABOUT some of the research and
organizations discussed in this book, visit the following Web sites:

Ashoka: www.ashoka.org

Council on Foundations: www.cof.org

Dress for Success: www.dressforsuccess.org

Echoing Green: www.echoinggreen.org

Foundation Center: www.foundationcenter.org

GrantCraft: www.grantcraft.org

Independent Sector: www.independentsector.org

Internal Revenue Service: www.irs.gov

Musicians on Call: www.musiciansoncall.org

According to the Foundation Center's online directory, the
following foundations fund organizations and projects that seek to
advance the field of philanthropy and the nonprofit sector:

Bill and Melinda Gates Foundation (www.gatesfoundation.org)

Charles Stewart Mott Foundation (www.mott.org)

The David and Lucile Packard Foundation (www.packard.org)

The Ford Foundation (www.fordfound.org)

Heinz Endowments (www.heinz.org)

The James Irvine Foundation (www.irvine.org)

Kellogg Foundation (www.wkkf.org)

Lilly Endowment (www.lillyendowment.org)

Surdna Foundation (www.surdna.org)

The William and Flora Hewlett Foundation (www.hewlett.org)

ACKNOWLEDGMENTS

WHEN WE STARTED ON THIS JOURNEY, we had no idea that it truly would take a village to complete the task. We are grateful to those we list here and many others over many years who have helped us assemble the viewpoints that we present here only as our own.

First, we owe a debt of gratitude to our partner and collaborator, the writer John Sedgwick, who came into this project as a new colleague and is leaving it as a good friend. He helped us capture our thoughts and blend two distinct voices into one—no easy task, either one, but the result is this book. We are ever grateful.

Our colleagues at the Andrea and Charles Bronfman Philanthropies continually impress us with their dedication and their ability to teach us something new every day. A number of them offered trenchant comments on this work. We very much appreciate all of their efforts, but especially the reviews, suggestions, nudges, and assistance of Roger Bennett, Sharna Goldseker, Jason Soloway, Ann Dadson, and Janet Aviad. We also thank Roger and the team for the postwriting activities. Yvonne Deery's copious research exceeded our fondest hopes, as did her unfailing eagerness, promptness, and good cheer. John Hoover provided great guidance on all things financial. We are also grateful to our long-standing assistants, Angela Forster and Barbara Plotnick, without whom neither one of us could get anything done. Our heartfelt thanks to them both.

The memory of Andrea Morrison Bronfman is embedded in virtually every page of this book, explicitly cited in many of the anecdotes that we include. She always strived to make people better than they were. Individually and together, we were no exception. We miss her.

We are grateful to our editor, Karen Murphy, and all her colleagues at Jossey-Bass, especially Erin Moy, Mary Garrett, Cynthia Shannon, and Cedric Crocker, who have been so competent and gracious through this process, as well as to our agent, Kate Lee, and the ICM team, who guided us so very well.

Our beloved wives, Bonnie Roche-Bronfman and Audrey Weiner, are extraordinarily talented and supportive women whose imprint is continuous throughout this volume. They enrich the lives of many, and we are grateful to be the full-time beneficiaries of their essence.

Finally, we wish to acknowledge the many nonprofit professional and volunteer leaders who have taught us over the years. Brilliant, devoted, impassioned: they are the source of most of the book's wisdom. Any failings are completely our own.

Charles Bronfman
Jeffrey Solomon

ABOUT THE AUTHORS

CHARLES R. BRONFMAN IS CHAIRMAN of the Andrea and Charles Bronfman Philanthropies, which he created with his late wife in 1985. He has had several careers, many at the same time. He joined the Seagram Company in 1952, a business founded by his father, Samuel Bronfman. He began as a trainee and moved up the ranks, holding such titles as president of the Canadian Subsidiaries and liaison officer to the Dupont Company. Shortly after the formation of Vivendi Universal in December 2000 and coinciding with his fiftieth anniversary of employment at Seagram, Bronfman, then co-chairman of the company, retired from the business. In 1968 he became the principal owner of the Montreal Expos, a position he held until 1991, when the club was sold. It was the first major league baseball team to exist outside the United States.

Bronfman began his philanthropic career at the age of seventeen. He was president of the Montreal Federation from 1973 to 1974. He joined the board of CLAL (Center for Learning and Leadership) in 1992 and was its chair from 1998 until he was named founding chair of the United Jewish Communities in 1999, a post he held until 2001. He currently sits on the boards of trustees of Mount Sinai Medical Center (New York City), Brandeis University, and Village Academies (New York City) and is a member of the International Council of Hillel. Included in his honors was making the first ceremonial pitch at the World Series in Toronto in 1992, the first such contest ever to be played outside the United States. He became a member of the Queen's Privy Council for Canada and a Companion of the Order of Canada, the highest civilian honor in that country. He, with his late wife, Andrea, was awarded honorary citizenship of Jerusalem. Bronfman holds honorary degrees from several universities located in Canada, the United States, and Israel.

—᧱⟶

Jeffrey R. Solomon is the president of the Andrea and Charles Bronfman Philanthropies, a group of foundations operating in Canada, Israel, and the United States. Among the foundation's innovative launches are Birthright Israel, a program bringing hundreds of thousands of young adults to Israel for a ten-day trip; the Gift of New York, a powerful response to the terrorist attacks of September 11, 2001, helping to ease the suffering of the families of victims through the healing power of culture; and Project Involvement, an educational reform program serving some 265,000 Israeli elementary school students.

Solomon has also served as senior vice president and chief operating officer of UJA-Federation of New York, president of Altro Health and Rehabilitation Services in New York, and associate executive director of both the Miami Jewish Home and Hospital for the Aged and the Miami Jewish Family and Children's Services. Solomon also served with the New York City and New York State governments, as well as with the federal government in Washington, D.C., and its regional offices in New York and Atlanta. An author of over eighty publications, he has been an adjunct associate professor at New York University and a lecturer at the University of Miami Department of Architecture and Columbia University School of Business. He has had academic clinical appointments from six universities in four states. He has served on numerous nonprofit and foundation boards including the FJC, a community foundation in New York, and the Council on Foundations, where he chaired the Committee on Ethics and Practice and served on its executive committee. He is a founding trustee of the World Faiths Development Dialogue and has received a number of honors from professional associations and universities.

Index